IB HISTORY
Internal Assessment

IB HISTORY
Internal Assessment

The Definitive History [HL/SL] IA
Guide For the International Baccalaureate [IB] Diploma

Ian Lourenço

Zouev IB Diploma Publishing

Published 2023

Printed by Zouev IB Diploma Publishing

ISBN 978-1-9163451-5-7, paperback.

TABLE OF CONTENTS

PART I
THE IB HISTORY IA GUIDE

1. INTRODUCTION TO THE HISTORY IA

If you have decided to open up, and read this book, it is likely that you fall within the following spectrum: You either know exactly what you want your IB History Internal Assessment (IA) to look like, and just want guidance, or you have no idea where to begin. Either way, you will find something useful within the content of these pages. Aside from seven, outstanding and high scoring History IAs that you may use as models or inspiration, this Guide will also include an introductory section containing a multitude of tips from deciding your topic to citing sources that will help maximise your score.

Now, more than ever, scoring highly on the IA is imperative for any IB student aiming for a 6 or a 7 in IB History, and a high overall score of 37+. Noticeably, as a result of the COVID-19 pandemic, students' overall performance in the International Baccalaureate became ever more reliant on how they scored on their IAs. Whether students took the exam or non-exam route, the straits of asynchronous, or online learning, inevitably hindered students ability to absorb the already-dense content of IB History, and other subjects too. Hence, for many, the Internal Assessment really became the determining factor of whether a student fell within one markband or the next.

As such, the History IA should not be overlooked, as it really can be the difference between a 4 and a 5, or a 6 and a 7. Yet this should not stun nor discourage you. In fact, it should serve as inspiration. Why? Because *You* are in control of your IA - from the beginning to the end. We all have had those moments in exams where our nerves tip over, our minds go blank, and it can be difficult to truly show all we know on the exam paper, even if we have studied hours at a time. But this is not something you should fear with the IA, especially having this Guide, because you have the power to make it the best it can be.

So, let us begin by answering the most basic question of them all: What exactly *is* the History Internal Assessment?

In essence, the History IA is an investigation of a historical topic of your choosing, in which you will learn how to tackle historical inquiries like a professional historian and reflect on the skills you employed. It is a completely self-guided investigation, meaning that although you must meet the structural guidelines of the IA, it can be on any historical topic you would like; you may even choose to do it on a topic that you have not directly studied in class. Although, I will later discuss how you should decide on whether you write your IA on a topic you have already been studying or not. In reality, the only requirement regarding the topic of the IA is that it should fall under a timeframe, which you should confirm with your teacher.

The IA should be **no longer than 2,200 words**, and it is divided into three sections. Section A is the identification and evaluation of sources, it should be around 500 words long, and it is where you will evaluate the values and limitations of two historical sources you utilised in your research, with reference to each source's origin, purpose, and content. Section B, the investigation, is approximately 1,300 words long, and is where you will attempt to answer your research question by employing evidence and integrating it with very clear critical commentary that leads the reader to an evidence-based conclusion. Lastly, Section C is your reflection, it should be roughly 400 words long, and this is where you will discuss how you faced the methodological challenges professional historians face, whilst writing your investigation, and how you overcame them. Later in this Guide, we will go over each section individually, and some specific pointers on how to maximise your marks in each.

The structure of the IA is exactly the same for HL and SL students, as both are worth 25 marks, with an available 6 marks for Section A, 15 for Section B, and 4 for Section C. However, the IA is worth 25% of the final grade for SL students and 20% for HL students, meaning that it is a significant portion of students' final grade. It is also worth noting that although the grade boundaries shift around from year to year, if you are striving for a level 7 in your IA, you should aim for at least 20/25 marks to ensure that you are well within the markband. As previously stated, the IA is a hefty portion of HL and SL students' final mark, which is why successfully securing a high score in it will place you on a good path to achieve a high overall mark in the subject.

Finally, it is also crucial to stress that writing the history IA is an intense, time consuming process, and that your final grade will amply be a reflection on the amount of time you dedicate to researching, writing, and improving it. In reality, the IBO recommends that at least 10 hours should be allocated to the Internal Assessment at both SL and HL. This estimate, however, mainly accounts for in-class time that your teacher will allot to explain the IA, review preliminary outlines, answer questions, and even to allow you to research and write. Still, it is worth keeping in mind (and this is perhaps my first advice) that you will, and should dedicate an additional 5-10 hours of your own time to writing your IA - especially if you are aiming for high marks. It is crucial that you understand this early on in the process so you may begin preparing, afterall, more hours dedicated to your IA are less hours you could be spending revising for another subject, taking a well-deserved break, or even writing another IA. Yet, do not let this startle you, and just remember: time management is key! As we move through this guide, you will find more tips to help you organise your time effectively, and ensure that you are working on your IA as much as you possibly can.

2. FINDING AND CHOOSING A SUITABLE TOPIC

Ensuring that you select a good, rich, and plentiful topic is crucial to writing an excellent IA. This, however, can be a stressful activity, given that the topic can truly "make or break" the IA. Yet, in this section I will provide a variety of tips that will help you select the perfect topic for you, and will reduce some of the anxiety of getting it right. Specifically, I will be covering how to balance between passion and availability of information, and how to potentially integrate the IA with other assessments you have to complete during the IB, through a concept I call "overlapping research".

As aforementioned, according to the IBO's guidelines for writing the IA, you are expected to come up with your IA topic by yourself. However, your topic must fall within a stipulated time frame set by the IBO. With that said, I would advise you to steer away from choosing topics that fall too close to the extremities of this timeline - topics that are too ancient, or very recent. This is mainly because you will likely face a lot of challenges with effectively finding credible and useful sources for your research, either because many have been lost through time, or are yet to be revealed. For instance, if you choose to write your IA on ancient Egypt,

3200-3000 BCE, whilst you might be able to find an array of secondary sources, you will most definitely have a hard time finding strong primary sources to employ in your work, as the few writings that have been uncovered from that period are hard to interpret, even by professional archeologists and historians. This can damage your IA, as you would fail to balance between primary and secondary sources. Similarly, if you decide that your topic will be the 2001 9/11 terrorist attacks in the USA, you will find that many valuable government archives that could have enriched your research are still classified, and thus out of your reach. Hence, look for topics that comfortably fall within this timeline, as these will be where you will most definitely find a range of sources to explore.

Being mindful of this, you should also remember that the IA is your opportunity to explore any historical topic you like, and you should definitely take advantage of this. We all know what it is like to study our favourite topic in class, and to be extremely excited to learn more about it. Yet, we also know how dull and boring some topics can be, so much so that flipping the next page of the textbook can be a challenge in itself. So, you should strive to find a topic more like the former than the latter. Remember, your topic does not have to be something that you have covered in class as part of your IB History curriculum, meaning that this is your chance to write on something you are truly passionate about. Take me as an example: Although I was fond of the topics I was covering in class, which mainly orbited around European history, I saw the IA as my chance to explore other areas of history that I never had the chance to study in an academic setting. Consequently, being a huge fan of "Hamilton: An American Musical" by Lin Manuel Miranda, I decided to write my IA on the political foundations of the United States, even though I had never explored the topic beyond the musical. This truly made the IA writing process more engaging, and motivating, as I managed to turn the laborious process of writing a 2,200 word investigation into an intellectual endeavour. If you can find a topic that excites you to a similar degree, you will definitely be able to overcome the struggles of writing with more ease, as you will not feel like you have to write the IA - you will want to.

Having said that, whilst I wholeheartedly believe that finding a topic that you are passionate about is crucial for your success, you must also be pragmatic with your topic selection by effectively balancing between passion with the availability of information. For instance, if you write on a topic that you are extremely passionate about but has poor availability of information, you will find that you will be driven to find and analyse new sources, yet this will quickly fade, as you will become increasingly frustrated with spending hours online or at the library, just to find few, mildly useful sources. On the contrary, if you opt for a topic that possesses a lot of information but does not interest you at all, you will find yourself mindlessly reading dozens of tedious articles, and books, whilst being unmotivated to write your work. Evidently, these are just a couple of the hindrances you will face if improperly balancing passion and efficacy, but they truly highlight the importance of selecting a topic that is interesting enough for you, but that also gives you a range of sources, and historians to work with.

You are probably wondering: How do I balance between passion and the availability of information? Well, this is a valid question, and the answer will shift from student to student. Yet, perhaps the most valuable answer to it comes with a rather upsetting truth: there is no such thing as the "perfect" topic. Frankly, understanding this is the first step to effectively finding a topic that is most suitable for you, depending on the type of student you are. Broadly speaking, if you are a student who truly enjoys studying history (considering it one of, if not your favourite subject), you might be better off choosing a topic that extensively excites you, whilst slightly lacking information. This is mainly because, although you will have to work harder to find useful, informative, and credible sources, you will be able to keep yourself motivated throughout the entire process; more so than if you had chosen a topic you find dull, but that gives you a lot to work with. Being a history buff myself, I trailed this very path, as even though the topic I chose was fascinating to me, there was a limited amount of relevant information on it. Yet this did not frustrate nor dishearten me, as my curiosity was a drive in itself. But not everyone considers history one of their favourite subjects, and if that applies to you, perhaps being more pragmatic and selecting a topic that possesses a lot of information, but only somewhat interests you might be best. Realistically, if you are going to find the process of writing the history IA tiresome anyway, you might as well ensure that you are at least writing it on a topic that you will not struggle to research. Doing such may reduce some of the stress of writing the IA, hopefully allowing you to move through it a little more easily. Still, I must stress, by no means should any student completely sacrifice passion for the availability of information or vice-versa, as finding the sweet spot between these two concepts is key for your motivation, and the writing of a well-researched history IA.

Now that I have covered what you should be mindful of prior to selecting your topic, let me provide you with some tips on how you should go about researching topics. Unsurprisingly, the first important step is to brainstorm potential topics, and you can easily do so by recalling areas of history that have caught your attention in the past, but also by recollecting movies you have watched, and books you have read. Remember, your first understanding of what topics you might want to do the IA does not have to be very deep, you can just jot down ideas and keep them in mind. Referencing back to my example, I decided to write my IA on the political foundations of the United States after watching a musical, which is proof that inspiration may really bloom from anywhere. Try to think of 5-10 topics you would like to explore, and try to diversify these across a wide range of fields in history, so you have different ideas to draw upon.

Next, start doing some preliminary research around the topics you have selected. Read articles, chapters of books (often the introductions and conclusions provide valuable nuggets of information), YouTube videos, movies, and any other medium that may enhance your understanding of a given topic. At this point you can start thinking of historical themes, issues, people, and events that spark your curiosity, and could potentially lead to a solid topic. This preliminary research is also of great importance for two main reasons. Firstly, you will get a sense of what topics truly interest you, and by doing research, you will begin to be mindful of how much information there is available on that topic - this helps with the "balance" discussed above. Secondly, you will be able to slowly increase the specificity of your topic, as you will have started from a large idea but will now look at what exactly interests you within that topic, which will help you come up with a research question later on. Make sure to keep track of the sources you come across as you do your preliminary research because if you end up choosing that topic, you will not need to scram through the internet trying to find those sources again.

Finally, although I have strongly advocated for you to select any topic that interests you , it is also worth considering writing the IA on a topic you have, or will cover in class. There are countless advantages to doing this, but the main one is that doing so will allow you to benefit from a concept known as "overlapping research". This basically means that as you research for your IA, you will indirectly be revising for a topic in your history curriculum. This can be a clever thing to do as you will be fulfilling one of the requirements of the IB History course, whilst simultaneously becoming more knowledgeable on a topic that you will likely use in one of your history assessments. This option can be especially helpful for students who are not very fond of history, as they may supplement the research of their IA with the content covered in class, and vice-versa.

3. WRITING A RESEARCH QUESTION

Having selected your main topic, now it is time to come up with your research question, which will dictate the scope of your whole investigation. For this reason, it is extremely important that you formulate a question that proposes the exact discussion you will make. This may seem like an obvious statement, but one of the main reasons students lose marks on the history IA is because they fail to understand the scope of their question, and conduct an investigation that lacks focus; ultimately leaving their research question unanswered. For this reason, in this section we shall discuss how you can identify what you would like your research question to address, how to properly word your question, and how to ensure your question is not too specific nor too broad.

The first step to writing a solid research question is to narrow down what exactly interests you in the topic you have selected. Your preliminary reading (discussed in the previous section) will help you achieve this, as you will begin to notice specific time periods, historical figures, and general factors (political, social, economical, etc.) that spark your curiosity about a topic. However, aside from these notions that are specific to your given topic, another great way to narrow down your interests is to utilise the key concepts for the IB History DP. You are unlikely to know what these are, as schools rarely stress their importance, but according to the IBO, they aim to "encourage students to engage with multiple perspectives and to appreciate the complex nature of historical concepts, issues, events and developments". In all, there are six of these concepts: change, continuity, causation, curiosity, significance, and perspectives. You can use them to identify what you would like to investigate within your topic. The table on the next page briefly explains what each of these concepts refer to, and shows some typical prompts associated with each.

Concept	Explanation	Typical question prompts
Change	Refers to changes to the status quo as a result of this topic.	→ What changes resulted from this topic? → To what extent did this event/person/issue cause change?
Continuity	Refers to how this topic maintained the status quo.	→ To what extent did this topic remain the same? → Did this event/person/issue cause progress or decline?
Causation	Refers to the causes that led to the occurrence of this topic.	→ What were the long-term, short-term, and immediate causes of this topic? → What were the factors that caused the event related to this topic?
Consequence	Refers to the impacts and effects of this topic.	→ What were the immediate, and long-term effects of this topic? → How significant were the effects of this topic?

Significance	Refers to how significant this topic, or the people involved, were at the time.	→ To what extent is this topic significant? Is the significance of this topic justified? → What events/ people/ issues are important to know about this topic?
Perspectives	Questions the specific perspectives, interpretations, and attestations about this topic	→ What different perspectives and interpretations are there about this topic? → How did people experience this topic?

Now that you have utilised your preliminary reading, and the six concepts of the IB History DP, you can begin to formulate your research questions. As previously stressed, this is an extremely important step, as your question will dictate the scope of your IA, and what you will focus on throughout your investigation. Consequently, if anything, remember this: wording matters. Use the IB command terms to ensure that your question is inviting the exact discussion you want to take place. Many of these terms appear to be similar, and that is because the difference between them is nuanced. Nevertheless, each term invites a different type of discussion, dictating a different scope to your IA, so you need to make sure you are using the correct one for you. Below, there is a table containing the best command terms you should consider; bare in mind there are more command terms (which you can find online), but I strongly advise you to use one of the ones below, as almost all of the high scoring IAs of recent years make use of them.

Command Term	What does it mean?
Analyse	Break down the topic to bring out its essential elements or structure.
Compare and contrast	Compare the similarities and differences between the events or people concerned, referring to both of them throughout.
Discuss	Critically propose arguments, and factors pro and against the prompt in question, in a balanced manner that leads to an evidence-based conclusion.
Evaluate	Make a critical analysis by weighing up the strengths and limitations of the different arguments concerning the prompt in question.
Examine	Scrutinise the merits and otherwise of existing arguments concerning a given issue.
To what extent/how far	Break down the merits and otherwise of the prompt in question, leading to an evidence-based conclusion that definitely answers the research question.

Once you have identified which command term best fits your investigation, you can finally write out your research question. More often than not, your question should include three components: place (where?), time (when?), and the main issue (what is being discussed?). These components will ensure that the specificity of your research question is enough, meaning that your question is neither too specific and limiting, nor too broad and vague. At this point, it is also worth mentioning that it is likely that your question will shift slightly throughout the course of your writing. As you deepen your research, and begin writing out your arguments, you might find that your investigation will tip in another direction than you originally expected, and so your research question might need to be tweaked. This is nothing to worry about, and you should be comfortable with making slight adjustments to your question to make sure it is coherent with the scope of your IA, as you write it out.

Finally, considering all of the information I have proposed, let us take a look at a couple of hypothetical research questions. Here we will evaluate how each question makes use of the key concepts for the IB History DP, the command terms, and whether they are good and appropriate questions overall. For the sake of comparison and simplicity, the questions will be about the same topic, so the differences between them can be understood clearly.

Example 1: What led to the failure of the Nazi economic policy during the Second World War?

Evidently, although this question has potential, it is far from a proper research question for a History IA. For once, it does not use any of the command terms, but rather employs the phrase "in what ways", which simply makes the question too broad. Indeed, there is some indication of the scope of the question, as the place (Germany), and the time (during WWII, 1939-45), are somewhat evident. However, the main issue (the failure of the Nazi economic policy) is only broadly stated, and does not give the question enough specificity. Nevertheless, it is worth noting that this question effectively uses the key concepts for the IB History DP, in specific, it is rooted in the "causation" concept.

This question could be improved by the inclusion of a command term, such as "how far" or "to what extent", and the inclusion of a specific time frame (1939-1945). Also, the main issue should be further specified, perhaps by mentioning a specific cause that led to the failure of the Nazi economic policy.

Example 2: To what extent was conscription the most effective way of reducing unemployment in 1935?

This question possesses some great elements to make it a perfectly structured research question. It makes use of a suitable command term, and it correctly identifies the time (1935), place (Germany), and the main issue (the use of conscription). Also, there is clear use of "significance" and "consequence" as the key concepts for the IB History DP. Nevertheless, this question is too narrow, and hence not a suitable research question for the History IA. Evidently, by limiting the scope of the question to the year 1935, this question prevents the investigation from exploring the effects of conscription (and comparing it to other policies) over the years. It is likely that one would face difficulties to find enough sources for this investigation, due to its excessively narrow scope.

A simple way to improve this question would be to broaden the scope of the question by broadening the time period concerned. For example, instead of simply exploring the year of 1935, the period of 1935-1939 could be analysed.

Example 3: Why did Hermann Göering's Four Year Plan (1936-1940) fail to effectively prepare the Nazi economy for the Second World War?

Similar to Example 2, this question is almost a perfect research question. It effectively highlights the time (1936-1940), place (Germany), main issue (the Four Year Plan), and makes good use of the "continuity" and "consequence" concepts of the IB History DP. The scope of the question is appropriate, not being too specific or too broad, and it seems as though the question would make for a good investigation. Still, there is one primary problem which is the exclusion of a suitable command term, given that this question begins with "why". More often than not, questions beginning with "why" can easily be made into "how far" or "to what extent questions", meaning that simply making this alteration would significantly improve this question.

Example 4: To what extent was investment in public work projects the most effective way of tackling unemployment in Nazi Germany, between 1933-1939?

This is a good example of a perfect, well structured research question. Evidently, it makes use of an appropriate commande term, and it clearly identifies the time (1933-1939), place (Nazi Germany), and main issue (tackling unemployment). Additionally, it is effectively rooted in the "significance" and "consequence" concepts for the IB History DP. This question also effectively invites the discussion of other factors used by the Nazis to tackle unemployment. This is because the question is rooted around "significance", as it asks if "investment in public work projects was ***the most effective way*** of tackling unemployment." Hence, in order to

22

effectively answer this question, other factors must be brought to the discussion, so that their significance can be compared to that of investment in public work projects. This type of question is what you should strive for when coming up with your own research question.

4. SEARCHING FOR SOURCES

We have briefly discussed the "preliminary research" stage of writing the IA, which mainly serves to help you get an overall understanding of the topics you might want to explore. In that stage, although you might have looked at academic and insightful sources, the bulk of your research will have been based on short articles and quick YouTube videos. However, this will not be enough when it comes to writing your IA. In this section, we will take a look at what sources you should include in your research, how to effectively make use of them throughout the researching and writing process, and where to find the best sources for your work.

According to the guidelines for the history IA, students must include a minimum of 6 sources in their bibliography, although it is likely that you will need more than that (personally, I used around 13 sources). These sources should be a mix of primary and secondary sources, and should also consist of various mediums, such as books, journals, etc. Being a History student, you are likely familiar with the difference between primary, and secondary sources, but it is worth reinforcing their distinction. Primary sources are any original sources of information (letters, newspapers, articles, posters, etc.) that were created at the time period you are studying. These sources can be great accounts of the perspective of specific people at the time, and the general depiction of the topic, which can enrichen your work to a great extent. Opposingly, secondary sources are any source of information produced after an event has taken place that discusses or opines on original accounts of said event. Secondary sources are extremely useful in your research, especially as you dive into the historiography of your topic by analysing the perspectives of different historians. It is extremely important that there is a balanced quantity of primary and secondary sources, as this will not only show the IBO that you have gone into great depth of research on your topic, but will also enable you to construct an investigation that effectively uses the merits of the different types of sources.

Although most students understand the difference between primary and secondary sources, many often struggle to find useful, and most importantly, credible sources. For this reason, below I have included a list of some of the best resources you can use to find sources. Although most of these resources are all online (and thus easy to access), they provide an array of mediums, including books, websites, journals, and academic papers that will help you diversify your bibliography.

Resource	Description	Sources you will find
Jstor	Jstor is an online academic library that includes about 2,000 academic journals, but has also recently branched out to include books and primary sources. The only downside to Jstor is that most content is paywalled, meaning a subscription is required to access the full platform. *Many schools often possess a subscription (or are willing to make one), so you should reach out to your advisors if this interests you.	Primary and secondary sources. Academic journals, books, and articles.
Google Scholar	Google Scholar is a free search engine that will help you tailor your research to an academic setting. Unlike standard Google searches, which lead to any existing URL, Google Scholar ensures that all results of your searches are educational and academic.	Mostly secondary sources. Academic journals, books, abstracts, and other scholarly literature.
University databases	Often overlooked, university databases are great resources to find academic papers. Often, it can be hard to analyse dense books and articles, so turning theses and investigations (which are formatted similarly to an IA) can be very insightful.	Mostly secondary sources.

		Academic papers, theses, dissertations.
	The only negative aspect of these databases is that they can be difficult to find online.	
Government Archives	Like university databases, few students turn to government archives as potential resources. However, these are incredible when it comes to finding original accounts of a specific topic. Still, these archives can be overwhelming to investigate, given the quantity of sources available.	Mostly primary sources. Government reports, and abstracts.
Open Online libraries	These are free online libraries that allow you to download an array of resources that are otherwise paywalled, or not digitised.	Mostly secondary sources. Academic journals, books, textbooks, and articles.

5. USING SOURCES EFFECTIVELY

As you move through the research stage of your IA, you must effectively make use of your time by properly analysing, and keeping track of all of your sources. In this section, I will provide some tips on how to best analyse any source you come across, and how to organise your sources in a productive manner. It is important to point out that the tips in this section will mainly target how to functionally extract content from your sources; in later sections I will dive into more concrete tips to help you evaluate your desired sources for Section A of the IA.

The key to successfully using your sources is to ensure that you are always actively engaging with the content you are consuming, rather than passively reading through it. This means that whenever with a source in hand, you should be taking notes, and start thinking of potential arguments you could make in your IA. Whether you choose to digitally annotate your sources on a document, directly take notes on a PDF version on a tablet, or even print out your sources and use a pen and highlighter, you must ensure that you are always being mindful of 3 things:

Firstly, you must highlight your sources mindfully. When going through sources (particularly books and articles), it can be tempting to excessively highlight extensive sections of text, as everything appears to be extremely useful. Immediately, you will find that this will not be a major issue, but in the long-run, once you revisit your notes, you will be extremely frustrated to find complete paragraphs, if not pages highlighted, as you will have failed to pinpoint what is truly relevant in your sources. To avoid this, you could limit yourself to highlight only a certain number of lines per page, as that will force you to be meticulous about what sections you are choosing to highlight. Also, try to limit highlights to potential quotations you might want to include in your IA, or specific historiographical perspectives.

Secondly, you must jot down your own thoughts as you go. This might seem obvious, but students often go through their sources with a highlight in hand, but not including any notes on the margin. This is a critical mistake, as you will find that once you re-read your "annotated" sources, the highlighted sections will be virtually worthless, as there will not be any ideas attached to them. Hence, ensure that whenever you highlight a piece of text, you also note your thoughts about it, and maybe even the reason why you chose to highlight it. Another good practice is to include a brief bullet point summary at the end of a page or chapter on what you just read; future-you will be thankful for this, as it makes it easier to find specific pieces of information. Later on, you will find that these quick notes will be the building blocks of your major arguments, so ensure that you are not overlooking them.

Finally, you must organise your sources. This is perhaps the most important point, as keeping track of your sources is indispensable in ensuring that your ideas are well developed and interconnected. There is nothing more frustrating than remembering an excellent point, or quotation to include in your work but not knowing where you saw it last, which forces you to desperately scram through all of your sources with the hopes of finding it again. Hence, ensure you are keeping track of your sources, and the ideas found within each. The best way to do this is to compose a "source table", as not only will this allow you to organise your sources, but it will also help you quickly, and functionally find any important points or quotations you may come across. There are countless ways of composing a source table, but the template below is the one I found to be most useful, as it accounts for the most necessary information you might need.

Source	Author	Type	Primary/ Secondary	Page number	Quote/ Point	Argument/ Analysis	What factor does it fall under?

To finalise this section, I will also provide some tips on how to use your time properly when annotating and finding sources. As this is perhaps the most laborious and time consuming stage of writing the IA, it is extremely important that you sort through your sources quickly, but also attentively. For this reason, when it comes to reading through sources, I recommend that (if the source is too long), rather than reading its entirety, target its introduction and conclusion. This is because these sections will provide you with a brief, yet useful, overview of what is accounted for in the source, which can save you a lot of time. Rather than spending time reading through a potentially worthless source, the introduction and the conclusion will allow you to rapidly judge whether the source could be useful to you, and worth your while.

Also, when using long books, theses or dissertations, focus on specific chapters rather than reading through the whole work. Not all sections of a source will be useful to you, and so it is best that you pragmatically find the sections/ chapters that are likely to possess the most amount of useful information.

6. DRAFTING AN OUTLINE

An often-overlooked stage of writing the History IA, drafting a thorough outline is crucial in ensuring that you have a great structure, and first draft for your IA. In this section we will go over some general tips to composing a good outline, and I will also provide a template of what I believe is the perfect outline for the History IA.

The outline is where all of the information you have gotten from your sources, and all of your ideas will come together in a coherent manner, and so ensuring that your outline is well-constructed is of utmost importance. Many students will often make a simple, half-page outline and call it a day, but this is an error that will only set you up for failure later on. Personally, I believe that you should make your outline as detailed as possible, as that will make writing your first draft much easier. Although it will be more time consuming to write an in-depth outline, this will be worth your while, as transforming your outline into a first draft will only be a matter of making the detailed bullet points into full sentences. Additionally, it is worth noting that, although your supervisor is only allowed to give you feedback on one draft of your IA, there is no official rule preventing supervisors from looking at outlines (as these are not yet drafts). Consequently, by making a very detailed outline and asking your teacher to make comments on it, you can receive slightly more feedback on how you can improve your points and arguments than you would by simply handing in a first-draft.

Hence, to help you build a meticulous and detailed outline, I have included below what I believe is the perfect structure to help you build robust, and well supported paragraphs. It is worth noting that this sort of structure is mainly applicable for Sections B and C of the IA (I will provide a sample structure for Section A later on), however, you may also use this outline template when planning other essays in your History class, and even other essay-based subjects.

For the introduction:

1. State your research question

2. Summarise the points/arguments you will make.

3. Briefly suggest where your investigation will lead to/what your conclusion will look like.

For your body paragraphs, structure every paragraph with the PSEESEEL structure:

1. Main point (1, 2, 3, ...)

    1. First sub-point (1.1, 1.2, 1.3, ...)

a.   First evidence (a, b, c, ...)→ using quotations, copy and paste the specific evidence you will use at this stage.

        1. First explanation of included evidence (i., ii., iii., ...)

1.2.   Second sub-point (1.1, 1.2, 1.3, ...)

    b. Second evidence (a, b, c, ...)→ using quotations, copy and paste the specific evidence you will use at this stage.

        1. Second explanation of included evidence (i., ii., iii., ...)

1.3   Link→ provide a "mini conclusion" to your paragraph, tying your first and second subpoints to the main point of the paragraph.

For your conclusion:

1. Summarise the points discussed in your investigation.

2. Provide a definite answer to your research question.

3. Justify your answer using evidence and logic.

By following the structure above, you will break down each of your paragraphs to a great extent, ensuring that all of your points are supported with concrete evidence, and a thorough, analytic, and evaluative explanation. Evidently, this structure will help you visualise a chain of logic within each individual paragraph, and across your investigation as a whole, meaning that your work will always be substantiated with robust historical content. This structure, however, is a mere template for you to follow, so feel free to tweak and adjust it depending on how you would like to structure your investigation.

7. TIPS FOR YOUR FIRST DRAFT

Having completed your outline, now it is time to write the first complete (or almost) version of your Internal Assessment. As stated in the previous section, producing a good first draft is of great importance, as this is in the only version of your IA that your supervisor is allowed to comment on, and help you improve before you hand in your final version. Therefore, in this section we shall discuss how you can build the best first draft possible, as to maximise the amount of constructive feedback you may extract from it.

The first point to keep in mind is that your first draft should be as complete as possible, so you may receive as much feedback as possible. Unfortunately, many students see the first-draft deadline of the IA as a chance to slack off and procrastinate work. Afterall, this is not the *real* deadline for handing in the IA, right? Well, not quite. In fact, this sort of thinking is a form of self-sabotage, given that your first draft is your first, and only chance, of receiving constructive criticism on your work that will help you improve your final version. Consequently, I urge you to fight off those natural instincts of procrastination, and to treat your first draft as if it were your final one. By doing so, you will be determined to make it as complete, detailed, and good as it can be, thereby allowing your teacher to take a look at the best possible version of your IA, and help you make it even better. Think about it, if you only submit 70% of your IA as your first-draft, you will only receive feedback on around 70% of your work, meaning that you submit your final version with 30% of unimproved work. You will have virtually thrown away the chance to increase your grade by around 30%, which can be the difference maker between one grade or the next.

Furthermore, your first draft should resemble your final work as much as possible. Often, as the first draft deadline approaches, students who have not done much work will simply write down anything mildly coherent, and related to their outline and submit it. Again, this is another critical mistake because even though you will receive feedback on these sections, if you redraft them entirely, all of the feedback will be lost. Thus, making your first draft as upload-ready as possible will help you ensure that you will be able to constructively build upon the feedback you receive, and make the necessary improvements. If explicitly necessary, by all means rewrite paragraphs (or even entire sections), yet this should not be a common practice.

There are two major ways of avoiding the mistakes above. The first was highlighted in the previous section of this book: constructing a thorough outline that will help you preemptively organise your ideas, and build substantiated paragraphs. The second, is one of the most classic pieces of advice you will most definitely have heard: time management. I recognise how cliché it is to reinforce this notion, but truthfully, there is no way of constructing a worthy first draft without effectively managing your time. Noticeably, the mistakes above were mainly consequences of procrastination and slacking off, meaning that you can avoid them by ensuring that you have enough time to write your IA, without rushing. Below are a few tips on how you can productively manage your time, and you can use these tips throughout the entire writing process of the IA, and even when writing other papers.

Strategy	Explanation
Use a calendar	Using a calendar can truly help you organise yourself, in the IA process. Google Calendar is a great resource as it allows you to shift around tasks and create deadlines in such a way that you can keep track of upcoming work. The key thing about a calendar is that it must help you visualise your timeframe so you can plan accordingly.
Set personal deadlines	Writing a 2,200 word essay can be really disheartening, so you must break this down into more bite-sized, manageable tasks. Being mindful of your final deadline, you can create "mini deadlines" within the time you have to help you make continuous progress with your IA.

Take it one day at a time	The writing process is already stressful enough, so do not undermine your confidence by trying to do everything at once. Using the two strategies listed above you will be able to tackle this challenge one day at a time, limiting your amount of daily stress but maximising your progress.

Another great thing that will help you extract as much feedback and constructive criticism for your IA as possible is to get another History teacher, a friend, or anyone to read your first draft prior to handing it in. Ideally, another History teacher, or another IA supervisor, would be best, as they could give you specific feedback on how to improve your work as an IA. Truthfully, another pair of eyes on your first draft can be of great help and could amplify your feedback to a greater extent. Not only could this person catch spelling mistakes and slight grammatical inaccuracies in your work, but they could also help you improve the legibility of your IA - which is essential. As we are so engaged with our own work, we often skim through confusing, or poorly worded sentences believing that they make sense, when they are in fact incoherent and difficult to read. Hence, other people can help you improve the clarity of your arguments by rewording specific sentences, which is critical in making your work cohesive for examiners.

Concluding this section, a good outline is integrally tied to a good first draft, which is integrally tied to a great final version of your IA. Keep this "domino effect" in mind as you write your first draft, as it will give you the motivation and drive to make it the best it can be. Do not fall into the common, unproductive traps of rushing through or inattentively writing your first draft, as it is a major pillar sustaining the final success of your Internal Assessment.

8. TIPS FOR WRITING SECTION A

As noted in the introduction of this book, Section A of the History IA is the identification and evaluation of sources, meaning that it is where you will evaluate the values and limitations of two historical sources you utilised in your research. In this section of the guide, I will provide some tips on how you should select the two sources, how you should analyse these sources, and what the general structure of Section A should look like.

The first crucial step in writing a good Section A is ensuring that you have selected fruitful sources to evaluate. Although you can select two primary sources or two secondary sources, for most students, I would recommend evaluating one primary and one secondary source. This is because doing so will enable you to diversify your points, given that the values and limitations of primary and secondary sources are quite different. Additionally, you should be mindful that, according to the IBO, the sources evaluated in Section A should be academic sources (letters, journals, books, etc.) rather than visual sources such as posters and cartoons.

However, besides this explicit stipulation set by the IBO, there are two additional, unofficial guidelines that you should be aware of when selecting your two sources. The first is that you should select sources that you extensively referenced in your work. The whole point of Section A is for you to show awareness of the merits and shortcomings of your sources, allowing you to display sensibility in writing a historical investigation. Hence, dedicating Section A to evaluating sources that are rarely sighted in your IA may not be well received by the moderator, as it defeats the point of the section. The second guideline is that you should select sources that have clear, noticeable values and limitations. Selecting sources to which the values and limitations are hard to identify is a considerable mistake, as you will fail to find concrete points to make about each source, and will find yourself waffling through the section. Therefore, be cautious and attentive about which sources you select. In fact, another favourable piece of advice is to write Section A after having written Section B, as you will be able to revisit Section B and check which of your sources ended up being the most useful; these should likely be the ones selected for Section A.

Once you have selected your sources, you should find the values and limitations within each source, and you should do this by using the acronym OPCVL. You will have likely heard of this acronym in class, yet it essentially refers to how you must find the values and limitations for the origin, purpose, and content of each source. Values are elements of the source that increase its credibility, or further the quality or delivery of the information present. Contrarily, limitations are factors that call into question the truthfulness, validity, or value of a source.

To achieve the full 6 marks of Section A, you must provide at least one value and one limitation for each source's origin, purpose, and content. Which signifies that you need to make about 12 different points. This may seem daunting, but below I have included two tables that will help you achieve this. The first table includes key questions regarding a source's origin, purpose, and content which will help you identify its values and limitations. The second is a table where you can organise your thoughts about the potential values and limitations of a source.

Origin	→ Where did the source originate from?
	→ Who is the author/creator of the source?
	→ When was this source written?
	→ How may the author/creator's nationality and political beliefs affect the source?
	→ What perspectives are evident in the source?
	→ Are there any perspectives not present in the source, if so whose?
Purpose	→ Why was this source created?
	→ What did the author/creator hope to achieve with this source?
	→ Who/what is the target audience of this source?
Content	→ What information does the source reveal and conceal?

	→ What is the message of this source?
	→ How useful is the information present, and is it trustworthy/ reliable?

	Value	Why is it a value?	Limitation	Why is it a limitation?
Origin				
Purpose				
Content				

Once you have utilised these tables to organise your ideas, you can finally write up Section A. When doing so, it is imperative that you remember to be objective and concise to secure clarity, and ensure that you are not overextending the word count. As there are only 6 marks available for this section, you should not be spending more than 500 words on it, as that will hinder your ability to effectively develop the other two sections of your IA. However, simply stating the values and limitations of your sources are not enough to get full marks. In reality, aside from stating your values and limitations, you should provide a brief explanation of each to truly show the moderator your comprehension of the implications of these on your sources. This will allow you to increase the specificity of your points, ensuring they are not mere vague observations. Below are three examples to demonstrate how this could be done.

1. A value of the source's origin is that it was written in 1978, 33 years after the events that took place in 1945. This gives the source the benefit of hindsight, as the author is able to make use of evidence that was issued during, and after 1945 to construct his opinion and perspective.

2.   A value of the purpose of the source is that it is a meeting minutes aiming to summarise what was discussed between Churchill and Truman in the meeting of September 1945. Hence, the source pinpoints all of the relevant information, and exchanges between the two in a clear and concise manner, allowing the reader to quickly grasp the occurrences of the meeting.

3.   A limitation of the content of the source is that it provides constrained information on the hostilities of the British government towards a potential Nazi advance in November 1942. As the source was written whilst events were unfolding, most of this useful information was still classified, and hence unavailable to the public, which is why the source does not include any insights on this matter.

Also, you should be conscious of clearly organising your points in Section A. As you will be stating multiple values and limitations, with respect to two different sources, your writing can easily become confusing and unclear if improperly organised. Which is why finding a valuable structure is fundamental. Although there are various structures you could follow (as you will see in the IA examples later on), I recommend that you break down Section A into 4 major paragraphs: Source 1's values, Source 1's limitations, Source 2's values, and Source 2's limitations. Although extremely simple, this structure will allow you to evaluate one source at a time, thereby assuring that the moderator will not be confused as they read along, mixing up the values and limitations of both sources. There are other ways of securing clarity, such as by first discussing both sources' values, and then both sources' limitations; this should be fine too. Yet, I would advise you to refrain from intercalating between discussing the elements of source 1 and 2, as that can easily become unclear.

Lastly, I must not finish this section without warning you about one dire mistake students often make, which can cost 2-3 marks in Section A: to argue that a source's bias is a limitation of it. Contrary to popular belief, this is an erroneous assumption, as bias does not immediately discredit a source. In some sources, such as books, it can be very easy to identify the author's bias, whereas in others, such as textbooks, bias is more thoroughly concealed. Yet the reality is that all sources possess some degree of bias, after all they are all crafted by humans with different perspectives and beliefs. Consequently, you should attempt to demonstrate your awareness of a source's bias, and use this to discuss how it affects the content of the source. You can then make a case for whether the bias is a value or limitation of the source, but never solely cite bias as a limitation within itself.

9. TIPS FOR WRITING SECTION B

Undoubtedly, Section B, the investigation, is the most important part of the IA, as 60% of the available marks derive from it. Hence, understanding the ins and outs of this section is a must in order to secure a high overall score on the IA. In this section, we will go over the general structure you should aim to follow in Section B, and I will also provide some tips on how you can make it a stellar investigation.

Interestingly enough, the structure of Section B is not dissimilar to that of other essays you will have written in History class. This is a great advantage, as you will be familiar with what you must do. There are three indispensable components for a great Section B: An introduction, 3-5 body paragraphs, and a conclusion. In section 6 of this guide, I have already provided what I believe is the perfect structure that will allow you to develop these components into clear, evaluative, and analytical paragraphs. Evidently, you need to allocate a significant proportion of the 2,200 words available to develop Section B to the proper extent, as you need to make substantiated and intelligent arguments. For this reason, I recommend that Section B be around 1,300 words long, as that will provide you with sufficient space to comfortably develop your arguments and tie them up with a reasonable, evidence-based conclusion.

Although, in section 6 of this guide, I have also provided a sample structure for Section B's introduction, and conclusion, I must stress their importance. On the one hand, the introduction is fairly straightforward, as you simply have to ensure that you are clearly communicating to the examiner that you know what your investigation is about, which you will do by briefly introducing the factors that will be discussed, and also suggesting what conclusion your findings will lead to. On the other hand, and contrary to popular belief, the conclusion is slightly trickier, as it should consist of more than a brief summary of the arguments you have made in your investigation. Ultimately, the conclusion should be where you provide a definite, final answer to your research question. Naturally, this answer should coincide with and be supported by the arguments you make throughout Section B; meaning that your conclusion cannot stray from the path your body paragraphs have traced. Perhaps the worst mistake a student can make is to write an investigation that seems to suggest one conclusion, yet actually ends with a completely different determination. Not only does this make the conclusion unsubstantiated, but it also shows the examiner that you do not know the "throughline" of your investigation, and how your points are interconnected to lead to a final answer to your research question. For this reason, you should be extremely aware of the conclusion that your arguments suggest. Sometimes, you might find that your arguments lead to a different conclusion than you originally intended; yet you should not fight this, and rather follow your arguments naturally, even if your conclusion does not coincide with your personal views of the topic. Your conclusion must agree with your investigation, not with you.

Now, I will provide some general tips on how you can further the organisation, analysis, and evaluation of your Section B. The first of which is to use connectives throughout your writing. This may also seem like an obvious tip, but the difference connectives can make in improving the organisation and cohesiveness of your investigation cannot be understated. Connectives will help you build a "chain of logic" within each paragraph, and across each paragraph, as they enable you to clearly tie each piece of evidence and explanation, strengthening your arguments overall. By following the paragraph structures I proposed in section 6, and utilising connectives to improve the flow of your writing, you are guaranteed to build persuasive and effective paragraphs.

Additionally, it is crucial that you understand how to properly employ evidence (facts, statistics, perspectives) in your investigation. Erroneously, many students believe that inserting as much evidence as possible within their body paragraphs is the best way of supporting their points. However, this generally leads to work that is descriptive and narrative, rather than analytical and evaluative, which I will explain further later on. Truthfully, less is often more when it comes to using concrete evidence in your investigation. This is because you should input only the necessary amount of evidence to strengthen your points, and spend the majority of your time analysing and explaining such evidence to deepen your arguments. This can be a tricky notion to understand, so below I have provided two simple examples to help you visualise this. The first paragraph attempts to compensate for a lack of sophisticated analysis by excessively using evidence, whereas the second one employs evidence, and breaks it down through a thorough explanation that effectively supports the point being made. As these are mere examples, I have not gone into as much depth as I suggested in the paragraph structures presented in section 6, yet these are enough to show you how to not overuse evidence in Section B.

1. Mussolini attempted to portray himself as Italy's great leader by establishing a strong cult of personality. In 1926, he did this by repressing opposition newspapers and arresting journalists that spoke negatively of his regime and leadership. In parallel to suppressing opposition, Mussolini would use different mediums to massively spread his message, such as broadcasting his speeches through radio. Also, he implemented a fascist curriculum in Italy's public schools, in which he was depicted as the infallible saviour of Italy, often being referred to as "the new Caesar", and was portrayed as the "model Italian", a strong, athletic and courageous man.

2. Mussolini attempted to portray himself as Italy's great leader by establishing a strong cult of personality. Interestingly, fascist propaganda attempted to portray him in two different ways to convey different messages, at different times. On the one hand, Fascist propaganda attempted to portray Mussolini as an infallible man of culture that the people should look up to. Propaganda achieved this by spreading myths about Mussolini, such as claiming that he had read and memorised 35 volumes of Italian encyclopaedias. On the other hand, propaganda would also attempt to portray Mussolini as a man of the people to which the "average Italian" could relate to. Evidently, propaganda would often depict Mussolini driving tractors, ploughing land, and holding children; daily activities carried out by Italians. The effect of this duality in Mussolini's cult of personality was that Mussolini was able to construct different personas which he could adopt to appeal to the Italian people depending on what he needed to convey.

Furthermore, you should also be comfortable with employing historiography in your investigation to further support your arguments. You will have likely heard of the term "historiography" in your History lessons, but to summarise, it essentially refers to how History is written, meaning how different historians conceptualise History. Ultimately, the existence of historiography means that History is differently perceived by historians. For instance, with reference to a historical event, X, historian A might argue that factor C was the greatest cause of event X, whereas historian B might argue that the most significant cause of X was event D. You must include historiography in your investigation if you wish to score highly on Section B, as it deepens the sophistication of your arguments, showing the IA moderators that you are conscious of the academic debate around your selected topic. Overall, there are two major ways of using historiography in Section B. The first is to use the perspectives of historians that coincide with your own to give your arguments further credibility. Besides this, you will also strengthen the foundation of your ideas, afterall, they will be supported by renowned names in the field. The second way to employ historiography is to include an interpretation that diverges from your argument, and contest it using evidence and logic. If properly done, this can be an admirable element of your investigation that will pleasantly surprise the examiner. Afterall, you will be rebutting the perspective of an established historian, showcasing the solidity of your arguments. Below I have included examples for both of these tactics to help you further understand how they play out in practice.

1. Mussolini's attempt to transform Italy into a corporate state was an utter failure because of the power imbalances between employers and workers. This perspective is supported by the British historian Martin Blinkhorn, who claims that corporatism "disguised the exploitation and oppression of labour". Evidently, as Mussolini was reluctant to lose support of big business, he gave business owners greater power to repress workers' rights, such as denying them paid holidays and intensifying working hours as they saw fit. Additionally, large Fascist Trade Unions were split into smaller groups, making them weaker, and hence their power to bargain with employers. Both of these examples expose how, under Mussolini's regime, employers had great control over production, whereas workers struggled to advocate for their desires and rights.

2.   On the other hand, some may argue that Mussolini managed to boost the Italian economy, and improve the living standards for all Italians. One of these people is the American historian Spencer Di Scala, who claimed that Mussolini managed to modernise and progress the Italian economy and that, under Mussolini, "Italy's profile began to resemble that of modern European countries to a greater degree than in the past." Truthfully, Mussolini did manage to grow the Italian economy to some extent, such as by increasing grain production to 7 million tonnes a year during the 1930s, in comparison to 5.5 million during the 1920s. However, the economic development of Italy still left thousands of Italians in poverty, and with a low standard of life. For example, Italian farmers and peasants attempted to escape Mussolini's ruthless agricultural policies by migrating to cities, so much so that the population of Rome doubled between 1921-41. Still, the situation in cities was also gloomy as the abolition of trade unions meant that workers suffered with low pay and long working hours; It is estimated the real wages fell by 10% between 1925-38. Consequently, although there are some merits to Di Scala's claim, the reality was that the economic improvement of Italy was not enjoyed by its population.

You should also be conscious of what not to do in Section B. The first element to be aware of is to avoid making your work descriptive and narrative. A common mistake by students is to describe historical events in their investigation, making their work seem like a textbook. This will extensively harm your grade in Section B, given that the point of the section is for you to be evaluative and analytical in order to construct your arguments. But this is easier said than done, as it truly takes practice to understand how to limit the narrative nature of your writing. For this reason, as you write out your paragraphs, you should recurrently ask yourself: Am I simply describing what happened or am I using evidence to construct my arguments? Often the difference between these two is nuanced, but you will become more comfortable with finding it in time. As previously mentioned, an effective way to limit description and narration in your writing is to employ only the *necessary* amount of evidence; remember, less is often more. This is because by only explicitly including evidence that helps you construct your arguments, you can refrain from rambling on about the events that took place and focus your arguments on developing your points. Another way to avoid being narrative is to embed historical context in your arguments and explanations, rather than bluntly regurgitating historical facts. This will allow you to include useful historical information in a delicate manner that complements your points, rather than overshadow it. Again, for you to better understand these notions, reference the examples below. The first example excessively uses historical facts, making the writing descriptive, narrative, and frankly, dull. In comparison, the second example surgically pinpoints evidence to support the argument being made, and embeds historical information within the explanation for contextualising purposes.

1. On June 30th 1934, in an event known as the Night of the Long Knives, Hitler ordered the purging of the SA paramilitary wing of the Nazi party, his political enemies and potential threats to his position. The purge was led by Hiendrich Himmler, and carried out by SS officials, who stormed inside apartments to kill and imprison anyone they had been told. In all, it is estimated that over 400 people were killed in the Night of the Long Knives, including some high profile individuals. Examples include, the leader of the SA, Ernst Rohm, and the former chancellor of Germany, Kurt von Schleicher.

2. Hitler safeguarded his position as Chancellor of Germany by diverting potential threats from spheres of power, and directly eliminating any danger to his personal position. An example of when he achieved both of these elements was on June 30th 1934, in an event known as the Night of the Long Knives. After discovering that Ernst Rohm, leader of the SA paramilitary group, planned to amalgamate the SA and the armed forces under his control to antagonise the army against Hitler, Hitler ordered the purging of the SA, and his other political enemies. Led by Hiendrich Himmler and his SS units, it is estimated that over 400 people were killed in the Night of the Long Knives. The purge allowed Hitler to cleanse the Nazi state from potential threats, which momentarily safeguarded his position as Chancellor, and protected his future endeavours in becoming Fuhrer of the country. Additionally, by carrying out the purge, Hitler sent a message to any potential threats that remained, exposing their fate should they attempt to undermine him.

Finally, the last thing you ought to avoid in Section B is vague and unclear writing. Again, this is another obvious observation, yet the reality is that many students do not know when their writing is vague, and hence are shocked to see their Section B score badly. Vague writing often makes use of general words such as "people", "things", "factors", "many", "etc", all of which could be easily replaced by actual information on the topic in question. The use of these words (without proper explanation) is often perceived by moderators as a message that the student does not know what they are talking about, hence the use of these imprecise words. For this reason, you must ensure that your writing is precise, which you should do by being specific with your words. Instead of "people", cite names. Instead of "many", cite numbers. And so on. Doing so will enable you to make your writing as detailed as possible, which will push your investigation to the higher mark bands. You should also avoid vagueness by certifying that every sentence in your paragraphs contributes to constructing your arguments, and most importantly, answering the research question. Not only does the inclusion of insubstantial statements make it seem like you are waffling, but they often obstruct your ability of building clear chains of logic in your arguments. Below, I have included examples to help you conceptualise this idea. The two paragraphs are virtually the same, except that the first one is full of vague writing, and purposeless sentences, whereas the second is composed of precise language that follows a chain of logic.

1. Hitler sought to encourage German women to have more children, as an attempt to increase the population of the Reich. One policy he implemented to achieve this was to provide married couples with marriage loans. These loans were sums of money that couples could receive, which aimed to encourage them to have children. However, to qualify for the loan, aside from being married, women had to renounce their employment. Still, many women were happy to do so, as they would receive money, and so many couples received marriage loans over the years. Still, these loans did not allow Hitler to achieve his goals, as the loan was not enough to cover the costs of raising a certain number of children.

2. Hitler sought to encourage German women to have more children, as an attempt to increase the population of the Reich. He believed women ought to supply the Third Reich with more Germans, so it could effectively expand across Europe, and dominate other nations. Hence, a major policy that Hitler implemented as an attempt to achieve this was the provision of marriage loans. These were 1000 Reichsmark loans to be paid at 1% interest that aimed to encourage married couples to have children, so much so that the interest rate of the loan decreased by ¼ per child the couple had. Additionally, to qualify for the loan, women had to

renounce their employment. The purpose of this was to discourage women from working, so unemployed men could take the jobs, but also so they could stay home and care for their children. In all, these loans were quite successful amongst married couples, as it is estimated that 42% of couples received the loan by 1939. Nevertheless, the loan was only partially successful in stimulating the birth rate of Germany. This was because even if a couple received the loan, it was still a financial burden to have more than two children, as the loan was not able to cover the costs beyond that.

10. TIPS FOR WRITING SECTION C

Section C, the third and final section of the history IA, consists of your reflection, where you will discuss how you encountered and dealt with the methodological challenges faced by professional historians, whilst writing your investigation. It is the section with the least amount of marks available, only 4/25, which means that you should spend around 400 words on it, as any more than that will inhibit you from developing Sections A and B to the necessary extent. In this section of the guide, I will provide some tips on how you can identify the methodological challenges you have faced, and how to build a thorough and intellectual reflection from them.

Often, students struggle with identifying the methodological challenges they have faced, yet the reality is that these are more common than we think. We come across these challenges unconsciously, and they are typically the hardest ones to overcome because they are mainly to do with how we write and research history. These can be basic hindrances, such as the difficulty with finding credible sources, but they can also be more complex ones, such as dealing with the numerous, and often opposing perspectives presented within different sources. Inherent biases, hindsights, how the time a source was written influences its content, are all examples of the challenges you may face when writing the IA. Ultimately, these limitations are all rooted in the fact that History is an evidence-based subject, so you should also demonstrate awareness of the nature of History, as a field of study, in coexisting with these limitations.

Yet, identifying these limitations are easier said than done. For this reason, it is essential that you remain aware of these potential challenges as you research and write your IA. Whenever you stumble upon an obstacle concerning your ability to use evidence and work with different perspectives, make sure to make a note of it, as it can be of great use when it comes to writing your reflection. To help you do this, below I have included some key questions that you should keep in mind as you move through your IA, as these will help you slowly build your consciousness regarding the methodological challenges you come across.

→ What is the role of the historian in writing history?	→ What is history, and why do we need it?
→ Can the historian ever truly be objective?	→ How are the methods historians used limited by their time, place, ideology, and political view?
→ How do we utilise different perspectives to construct history?	→ What are the implications of history being an evidenced-based subject, not reliant on new discoveries like scientific fields?
→ Are some perspectives more valid than others?	→ How does mass culture, media, and trends influence historical understanding?
→ What are the limitations with how historians determine causation and impact of historical events?	

Nevertheless, it is also important to stress that, in your reflection, you should demonstrate a clear understanding that the challenges you have faced are genuine challenges faced by historians. A frequent mistake students commit is to use Section C to ramble on about how hard it was to write the IA. Yet this is not what this is about. Professional historians also struggle with the evidenced-based nature of history, and the fact that their work is constructed on multiple accounts of a historical occurrence, each of which only partially depicts it. It is much like putting together a puzzle of a picture of a dog by using the pieces from multiple puzzle sets: You might get a picture of a dog in the end, but it will never look like a dog that ever truly existed. Hence, to assure that you are being mindful of actual challenges historians face (and that so have you), you might want to consider employing some historiography in Section C. These can help you communicate these challenges, and further show the examiner your understanding of the limitations of writing History. I would recommend that you check out *What is History?* by E.H Carr, as it is a great introduction to beginners on the limitations of historical writing and research, which will greatly help you when writing Section C. However, there are also other books which discuss similar notions such as *Historiography: An Introduction* by Eileen Chang, and *The Historian's Craft* by Marc Bloch which can also help you further grasp these ideas.

11. TIPS FOR CITING SOURCES

Citing sources is something that many students have a tendency to overlook, yet it is paramount that you understand how to do it well. The correct citation of sources in your IA is a requirement set by the IBO, and it is held to a high standard, as any uncited piece of work in your IA can be considered plagiarism, which could result in the immediate disqualification of your work. Additionally, it is simply a good practice for you to improve this skill whilst still an IB student, as you will use it extensively when in university. Consequently, in this section I will provide some tips on how you can organise your sources and correctly cite them in your work.

The first important step in ensuring that all of your sources are correctly cited is to keep your sources neatly organised throughout the process of writing the IA. I did mention the importance of this before, yet I must restress this idea, as you cannot lose track of where your sources are, and what information you are extracting from each one, as it will be extremely challenging for you to find yourself later on. Storing all of your sources into a single folder (digitally or analogically) so you always know where all of them are is a fair way of doing this. Yet, a more efficient way of organising yourself is to use some online citation generator platforms. Websites like MyBib, Scribbr, and Quillbot are all free citation generators, which will not only automatically generate your bibliography for you, but will also generate in-text citations in whichever style (Harvard, Oxford, etc.) you may need. Personally, I utilised MyBib to keep track of my sources and properly cite my work, but any of the other platforms listed above will serve you just as well.

Another great tip regarding in-text citations is to always cite your sources as you write, rather than doing it all at the end. I must confess that when writing my own History IA, I typed up my entire investigation, and only once the 2,200 words were finalised did I return to my document to input all of the necessary in-text citations that were missing. This is perhaps my greatest regret when I recall writing the IA, as it was incredibly difficult to remember exactly where I got the information from every paragraph and every line. I spent almost as many hours referencing my work as I did writing it. For this reason, I strongly recommend that, while writing the IA, whenever you input information retrieved from a source, make sure to make the in-text citation right then and there, or at least make a note of what source that information came from. Trust me, I know it is incredibly annoying to stop the flow of your writing to insert a reference (this was the reason I put it off in the first place), yet you will not regret doing so.

Finally, my last piece of advice when it comes to citing sources is that you should select a citation style by taking into account your word count. The IBO allows students to pick from a range of referencing styles to cite their IA, yet the most common ones are Harvard and Oxford referencing. The major difference between the two (and other styles as well), is that Harvard utilises in-text citations, whereas Oxford utilises footnotes. This difference may seem insignificant at first, but it is critical to remember that they will both impact the wordcount of your work differently. Specifically, Harvard's in-text citations will count towards your final word count (as they are embedded in your work), whereas Oxford's footnotes will not. This is why you should be attentive when selecting a referencing style. If you are confident that you will need the full 2,200 to properly develop, and complete your IA, using Oxford referencing is advisable, as you will not need to worry about your citations pushing you over the limit. On the contrary, if you feel that you will not go over the restriction, you might want to use Harvard referencing, as it is slightly simpler to employ. Either way, you must be aware of the magnitude of your work so you can select the referencing style that best suits you.

PART II
SEVEN EXAMPLES OF EXCELLENT
IB HISTORY IA

The IA featured in this section are all recently submitted IA that scored exceptionally well (band 7) after being moderated by the IBO. The IA are presented in the exact same way as they were submitted, without any edits or changes to formatting. We do not retain the copyright of these IA, nor is this publication endorsed by the IBO. The Internal Assessments are being re-printed with the permission of the original authors.

1. EXAMPLE ONE (23/25)

Title: How significant was the manipulation of Soviet youth in maintaining the communist ideology after the Russian Revolution? (1920-1930)

Author: Anonymous

Session: May 2021

Level: SL

Table of Contents

Identification and evaluation of the sources

This investigation will explore the following research question:

How significant was the manipulation of the Soviet Youth in maintaining the communist ideology after the Russian Revolution (1920-1930)?

The sources chosen for an in-depth evaluation are *"The Tasks of the Youth Leagues"*[1] (speech by Vladimir Lenin delivered at the third All-Russia Congress of The Russian Young Communist League in 1920) and *"The Whisperers: Private Life in Stalin's Russia"*[2] authored by Orlando Figes in 2007.

In the "The Tasks of the Youth League", Vladimir Lenin stresses the importance of the youth in building the future of the country and supporting the communist ideology. The origin of this source is valuable because it gives an insight into personal views and policies as it comes from Lenin himself- the leader of the Bolshevik revolution. Therefore, one can directly examine his view related to the significance of the youth and the tasks they should complete in order to support the newly founded society. However, because it's a speech, a limitation of the origin is that it does not offer an insight into the results and success of the youth, so one cannot measure its significance. It is also limited due to the tone, persuasive language, pathos, and subjectivity regarding Marxist beliefs.

The purpose of the speech was to motivate the revolutionary youth of Russia into completing their tasks given the struggle to maintain the regime after the Revolution. This is valuable since it indicates the importance of the youth for Lenin and the Bolsheviks and gives an insight into their ambitions and tactics at that time. The limitation both in content and purpose,

---

[1] Lenin V. (1920). *The Tasks of the Youth Leagues.* Collected Works, volume 31. Retrieved April 4, 2020, from https://www.marxists.org/archive/lenin/works/1920/oct/02.htm.

[2] Figes O. (2007) *"The Whisperers: Private Life in Stalin's Russia"*. Henry Holt and Company.

however, is that the speech was given to convince the youth about the communist views, which omits other methods that are significant for maintaining the regime.

"The Whisperers: Private Life in Stalin's Russia" is a historical book which investigates the repressive ways of indoctrination, the influence of the Soviet regime and its campaigns of Terror and propaganda on family relationships and youth. The purpose of the book is valuable in a way that it emphasizes the methods of repression and the role of the youth from an objective perspective. In addition, the value of the origin is that it was written by a historian- Orlando Figes who is an expert in Russian history. Likewise, being published in 2007, the source benefits of hindsight as the arguments are supported by a vast range of sources like letters, memoirs, and conversations.

However, the limitation of the content is that the book has a broad focus on the overall repression rather than only the youth and it focuses on a wide period (1917-1960). However, it is valuable that two chapters are mainly focused only on the control of education and methods of repression during 1917-1932, which provides views from different perspectives including the people's experience during that time.

Investigation

As the Russian Revolution in 1917 strengthened the Bolsheviks' political control over Russia, it was a necessity to implement several technics in order to maintain the new regime against all the threats and poverty. The main task was to transform the pre-revolutionary 'bourgeois' and tsarist culture into the proactive socialist forms of behavior and belief to indoctrinate the people into the communist collective way of life. Consequently, as the New Economic Policy was introduced in 1921, more focus was directed towards the educational creation of a new communist society[3] involving a social policy of moderation and discipline. Therefore, the youth were seen as significant for promoting the communist views throughout the future generations, breaking free from

---

[3] Gorsuch, A. E. (1992). *Soviet Youth and the Politics of Popular Culture during NEP*. Social History, 17(2), 189-201. Retrieved April 4, 2020, from www.jstor.org/stable/4286015

the contradictory pre-revolutionary beliefs and building a solid social hegemony. There are different perspectives upon the success and extent of significance compared to other methods, yet there is no doubt that the youth played a huge role.

Firstly, from a Marxist perspective, the youth were fit for the job mainly because they were easier to manipulate, they craved to become revolutionaries, be included, and this could be efficiently carried out through reforms in the educational system. For example, a schooling theorist[4] highlights the Bolsheviks' views on the importance of youth and the way they can be easily manipulated once they detach themselves from their parents and belong to the community. Consequently, the youth were important because they could be freed from the old beliefs, giving way to indoctrination and maintenance of the communist ideology.

Like emphasized in Lenin's speech[5], the implementation of Communist values was a guiding principle of the Soviet school curriculum and the role of Marxism in Soviet schools was as essential as the role of religion in old tsarist schools.[6] For instance, the post-Civil War children were encouraged to play at being revolutionaries. Soviet educational thinkers reinforced the structured 'learning through play' method through which the children could learn the Soviet values of collectivity, social activism and responsibility. Therefore, one of the main tasks of the Soviet school, as mentioned in Lenin's speech[7] was to instill collective obedience and the idea that the children had too a potential in becoming revolutionaries. Likewise, as observed through Figes' interviews, snitching, even on their own parents was highly encouraged, propagated specifically through the role model "Pavlik Morozov" who denounced his father to the party, thus inspiring the youth to emulate his achievement.[8]. In this way, the youth were highly significant for not only instilling communism in the future generations, but also helping the party to identify opposition and suspicious behavior.

From an orthodox perspective, the formation of the Youth Leagues such as the Komsomol and the Young Pioneers in 1918 played an important role as a mechanism for teaching the values of the CPSU to the youth, training them to become revolutionaries, and gaining voluntary help with

---

[4] Appendix 1
[5] Lenin V. (1920). *The Tasks of the Youth Leagues.* Collected Works, volume 31. Retrieved April 4, 2020, from https://www.marxists.org/archive/lenin/works/1920/oct/02.htm.
[6] Figes O. (2007). *The Whisperers: Private Life in Stalin's Russia.* Henry Holt and Company.
[7] Lenin V. (1920). *The Tasks of the Youth Leagues.* Collected Works, volume 31. Retrieved April 4, 2020, from https://www.marxists.org/archive/lenin/works/1920/oct/02.htm.
[8] Figes O. (2007) *"The Whisperers: Private Life in Stalin's Russia".* Henry Holt and Company.

building up the state[9]. The Komsomol, formally established as the youth division of the Communist party in 1918, primarily had to pose as a role model of "communist upbringing" and present the ideal communist worker through volunteering in various activities. They were expected to volunteer for the most devastating tasks such as helping with the harvest, enlisting for the new construction jobs, working in the mines, or going wherever the organization sends them.[10] They also played a key role in liquidating the Kulaks, reducing illiteracy and acting as shock brigadiers in the kolkhoz. In this way, they contributed significantly in industrialization, restoration of the economy, and thus helping maintain the rule[11]. By showing an example to the Pioneer youth, in March 1926, Komsomol membership reached a NEP-period peak of 1,750,000 members which rose to 3,00,000 in 1931 after the establishment of Stalin´s 5 year plan in 1928.[12] This emphasizes the effectiveness of luring the youth into to joining the collectivization and working for the Party without any profit beside recognition. However, a limitation of the respective view is that it is quite incomplete as it focuses only on the efficiency of youth, so it is not possible to measure its significance without comparing it to other methods used by the Party.

In contrast, some historians like Orlando Figes, Merle Fainsod and Oliver Lewis provide other perspectives on the efficiency of the youth indoctrination. The access to interviews with ex-Soviets gives an insight into how "the whole body of Soviet youth was ready to rise up in revolt against the communist regime at the first opportunity"[13]. For instance, their grandparents´ beliefs still consisted of old Tsarist ideals, and therefore there could be a collision between religious beliefs and the communist ideology taught in schools. The antipathy towards collectivization, all the hardship endured without measurable rewards, and the religious attitudes provoked some doubt towards the system which could not be annihilated through propaganda. Therefore, the

---

[9] Меркулов П. А. (2016). *ВКП(б) и комсомол в 1920-1930-е гг,* Управленческое консультирование. №11 (95). URL: https://cyberleninka.ru/article/n/vkp-b-i-komsomol-v-1920-1930-e-gg (date visited: 29.03.2020).

[10] Fainsod, M. (1951). *The Komsomols--A Study of Youth Under Dictatorship.* The American Political Science Review, 45(1), 18-40. Retrieved April 4, 2020, from JSTOR. doi:10.2307/1950882

[11] Никифоров, Ю. А. (2006) *Россия: иллюстрированная энциклопедия.* Москва: "ОЛМА-Пресс Образование", — C. 262. — 600 c.

[12] Bernstein, S. *(2013). Communist Upbringing under Stalin: The Political Socialization and Militarization of Soviet Youth, 1934-1941.* URL http://hdl.handle.net/1807/70050

[13] Fainsod, M. (1951). *The Komsomols--A Study of Youth Under Dictatorship.* The American Political Science Review, 45(1), 18-40. Retrieved April 4, 2020, from JSTOR. doi:10.2307/1950882

image of the Soviet Youth appears to be not that orthodox after all, at least not internally, so one cannot say that the manipulation of youth was entirely effective during that period.

Additionally, from a revisionist view, there were other significant factors that contributed towards the maintenance of the regime. For instance, without the use of terror and fear, the youth and everyone else would not have been forced to obey the rules and support the regime. Likewise, other tools such as the elimination of religion, various propaganda, labor camps, expulsion of intellectuals, and the "whip and carrot" strategy ensured the annihilation of any sign of overt opposition towards the regime. All these were presumably more important than the control of education, yet, the mixture of all of these made the biggest impact. This view proves valuable as it focuses on the wider picture rather than only on one factor, so it is more complete. However, because there was a lack of access to criticism due to censorship, the view is mostly based on testimonies and interviews which are not representative of the entire population's experience.

Finally, the youth manipulation was significant for maintaining the ideology throughout the future generations, instilling collective obedience and revolutionary behavior, helping with denunciation and elimination of the opposition and gaining voluntary help for industrialization or collectivization through the Youth Leagues. However, as discussed, this method alone would not have been effective without the application of other repressive tools. Likewise, even though there are testimonies showing how the youth were obeying, there are other contra arguments that explain how the youth were easy to rise up in revolt against the regime. Nevertheless, the indoctrination of youth was an invaluable method for the transition to the communist regime.

Reflection

Through this investigation, I certainly gained a valuable insight into the research methods used by historians, and thus the potential challenges that may arise throughout the process. This taught me that a historian should treat the facts as pieces of puzzle. In this, imagination is necessary to fit all those together and shape a meaningful representation of the past, which most of the time consists of gaps, making it incomplete. The methods used throughout the research included analyzing primary sources, investigating propaganda posters, reading books and monographs by different historians, presenting different points of view, and investigating sources in Russian as well.

Amongst the primary sources used, the interviews provided a significant insight into the way people from USSR perceived differently the effectiveness of the youth manipulation. Although eyewitness testimonies are not always reliable, by having more interviews that agree with each other, one can form a generalized impression about the subject. Additionally, gaining knowledge about the motifs from Lenin's speech also posed a challenge, since reading between the lines, watching the actual speech in Russian and interpreting the underlying purpose of the speech were necessary. Besides, for a historian it's an advantage to understand different languages, since by speaking Russian, I was not limited by other people's translations of primary source documents. However, a limitation of the primary sources coming from USSR is that they were often manipulated to shape the history differently during the years of Stalin's dictatorship, so there could be a problem with source reliability. Likewise, by coming from a post- Soviet country, I could not rely on what I've been taught in schools regarding this topic, so I had to make sense of it on my own.

Finally, unlike in science, we cannot exactly quantify the effectiveness of the manipulation of youth in maintaining the communist regime. Nevertheless, by analyzing the purpose for which they were used and the popularity of the youth leagues, we can come up with the conclusion the control of youth is indeed significant in the transition to a new regime. All in all, the knowledge gained from this topic can stress the problem that not only in the past, but also in the today's society, the manipulation of youth can be an abusive tool used by authoritarian leaders to promote and maintain their ideology.

included analyzing primary sources, investigating propaganda posters, reading books and monographs by different historians, presenting different points of view, and investigating sources in Russian as well.

Amongst the primary sources used, the interviews provided a significant insight into the way people from USSR perceived differently the effectiveness of the youth manipulation. Although eyewitness testimonies are not always reliable, by having more interviews that agree with each other, one can form a generalized impression about the subject. Additionally, gaining knowledge about the motifs from Lenin´s speech also posed a challenge, since reading between the lines, watching the actual speech in Russian and interpreting the underlying purpose of the speech were necessary. Besides, for a historian it´s an advantage to understand different languages, since by speaking Russian, I was not limited by other people's translations of primary source documents. However, a limitation of the primary sources coming from USSR is that they were often manipulated to shape the history differently during the years of Stalin´s dictatorship, so there could be a problem with source reliability. Likewise, by coming from a post- Soviet country, I could not rely on what I´ve been taught in schools regarding this topic, so I had to make sense of it on my own.

Finally, unlike in science, we cannot exactly quantify the effectiveness of the manipulation of youth in maintaining the communist regime. Nevertheless, by analyzing the purpose for which they were used and the popularity of the youth leagues, we can come up with the conclusion the control of youth is indeed significant in the transition to a new regime. All in all, the knowledge gained from this topic can stress the problem that not only in the past, but also in the today´s society, the manipulation of youth can be an abusive tool used by authoritarian leaders to promote and maintain their ideology.

Bibliography

Gorsuch, A. E. (1992). Soviet Youth and the Politics of Popular Culture during NEP. *Social History*, 17(2), 189-201. Retrieved April 4, 2020, from www.jstor.org/stable/4286015

Zenzinov, V. (1931). *Deserted: The Story of the Children Abandoned in Soviet Russia.* (London 1931), pp 27.

Никифоров, Ю. А. (2006) *Россия: иллюстрированная энциклопедия.* Москва: "ОЛМА-Пресс Образование", — С. 262. — 600 с.

Bernstein, S. *(2013). Communist Upbringing under Stalin: The Political Socialization and Militarization of Soviet Youth, 1934-1941.* URL http://hdl.handle.net/1807/70050

Fainsod, M. (1951). *The Komsomols--A Study of Youth Under Dictatorship.* The American Political Science Review, 45(1), 18-40. Retrieved April 4, 2020, from JSTOR. doi:10.2307/1950882

Lewis, O. (2007). *How much did the Bolsheviks need the Cheka and how well did they make use of it?* URL: https://www.e-ir.info/2007/12/02/76/

Lenin V. (1920). *The Tasks of the Youth Leagues.* Collected Works, volume 31. Retrieved April 4, 2020, from https://www.marxists.org/archive/lenin/works/1920/oct/02.htm.

Figes O. (2007) *"The Whisperers: Private Life in Stalin´s Russia".* Henry Holt and Company.

Меркулов П. А. (2016). *ВКП(б) и комсомол в 1920-1930-е гг,* Управленческое консультирование. №11 (95). URL: https://cyberleninka.ru/article/n/vkp-b-i-komsomol-v-1920-1930-e-gg (date visited: 29.03.2020).

Young *Communists in the USSR; A Soviet Monograph Describing the Demands Made upon Members of the Komsomol Organization.* Translated by Virginia Rhine. (Washington, D. C.: Public Affairs Press. 1950. Pp. 92.). (1951). American Political Science Review, 45(1), 253-253. doi:10.1017/S0003055400290321.

Gorsuch, A. E. (2004). Communist Youth Organizations. In J. R. Millar (Ed.), *Encyclopedia of Russian History* (Vol. 1, pp. 313-314). New York, NY: Macmillan Reference USA. Retrieved April 4, 2020, from https://link.gale.com/apps/doc/CX3404100289/WHIC?

Neumann, M. (2012). "Youth, It's Your Turn!": Generations and the Fate of the Russian Revolution (1917-1932). *Journal of Social History*, 46(2), 273-304. Retrieved April 4, 2020, from www.jstor.org/stable/23354132

2. EXAMPLE TWO (24/25)

Name: 'To what extent did proto-feminist movements during the French Revolution succeed in establishing sexual equality?

Author: Anonymous

Session: May 2020

Level: HL

Contents

Section 1: Identification and evaluation of sources

Source 1: (The British Museum, 2019)

"Cette fois ci, la justice est du côté du plus fort"

Source 2: (Bessiéres & Niedzwiecki, 1991, p. 14-16)

"DECLARATION OF THE RIGHTS OF WOMEN
DEDICATED TO THE QUEEN
1791

Article 1

Women are born free and are man's equal in law. Social distinctions can be founded solely on common utility.

Article 2

The aim of all political associations is to converse the natural and indefeasible rights of woman and man; these rights are liberty, property, safety and especially resistance to oppression.

Article 3

The principle of all sovereignty lies essentially in the nation, which is nothing more than the gathering of women and man; no body, no individual can exercise an authority that does not expressly emanate from that union

Article 4

Freedom and justice consist in returning all that belongs to others; as such the exercise of women's natural rights are only limited by the perpetual tyranny of men who oppose these rights; there limits must be reformed by the laws of nature and reason.

[...]

Article 7

No woman can be exempt; she can be accused, arrested and imprisoned in cases determined by law. Women, like men, obey this rigorous law.

Article 8

The law must establish only those punishments that are strictly and evidently necessary, and one can be punished solely under a law that was established and proclaimed prior to the crime and legally applied to women.

[...]

Article 10

No one should be harassed for her or his opinion, even the most basic beliefs; women have the right to ascend the gallows; they must also have the right to ascend to the tribune, insofar as their demonstrations do not trouble the public order established by law.

Article 11

The free communication of thoughts and opinions is one of women's most precious rights, because this freedom ensured the legitimacy of fathers toward their children. All citizen if the female sex can thus freely say: I am the mother of a child who belongs to you, without any barbarian prejudice forcing her to hide the truth, except in response to abuses of this right in cases determined by law

[...]

Article 17

Property belongs to both sexes united or separated; for each sex, property is a inalienable and sacred right; no one can be deprived of it as the true heritage of nature, except in cases where legally registered public necessity so requires, and unde the condition of a fair and prior indemnity."

This study will investigate the question: **To what extent did protofeminist movements during the French Revolution succeed in establishing sexual equality?** The first source I have selected for detailed analysis is a political cartoon published in 1789.[1] This source is particularly relevant to the investigation because it illustrates the relationship between the sexes, and the

---

[1] (The British Museum, 2019)

66

social classes, in the early stages of the Revolution. The second source I have selected is an extract of a declaration written by the political activist, Olympe de Gouges, in 1791.[2] This source is relevant to the investigation as it provides insight into the perspective of a central figure in the development of protofeminism.

Source 1 was created in Paris in 1789 by the artist A. P. Therefore, the origin of this source is valuable to the investigation because it can aid in forming a conception of the social unrest already present in France prior to the emergence of protofeminist movements. Secondly because the purpose of *source 1* is to express an opinion, it is valuable to the investigation, as this opinion may reflect that of the public. Finally, the content of *source 1* is valuable as it clearly depicts the unequal relationship between the social classes and sexes through visual means.

Nevertheless, *source 1* being from 1789, its origin is a limitation. The reason for this is that it cannot provide any information about the successes and failures of protofeminism throughout the Revolution. Additionally, the expressive purpose of the source is limiting the investigation because it is subjective, meaning that the source may not accurately represent the opinion of the public, but rather that of one person or group. This can also be seen in the content of the source, as it offers only one perspective on the relationship between the sexes in contemporary France, which is also a limitation.

---

[2] (Bessiéres & Niedzwiecki, 1991, p. 14-16)

67

Source 2 was written by Olympe de Gouges in 1791 as a response to the *Declaration of the Rights of Man and Citizen*. Because of this, the origin is a value, as the source provides the perspective of a contemporary protofeminist. Furthermore, as the purpose of the source is to affect both the public and the government, it is valuable to the investigation. This is because it provides insight into the form of society in which the protofeminist movements developed. Finally, the content is valuable to the investigation because it provides an idea of the state of sexual equality during the Revolution.

As for limitations, the origin of the source does not indicate whether the establishment of sexual equality was a success or not as the protofeminist movements had not yet fully emerged. Therefore, the origin is limiting the historical investigation. Secondly, the persuasive purpose of the source is a limitation. The source does not offer opposing perspectives - that of the state, for instance. Additionally, the content of *source 2* is a limitation because the historian has to imagine the political situation of women based on the indirect information in the declaration. For example, through the declaration that women are "man's equal in law", one would have to assume that de Gouges did not believe sexual equality to exist in 1791.

Section 2: Investigation

Although feminism did not develop until the nineteenth century, protofeminist aspirations were present during the French Revolution.[3] The extent to which the protofeminist movements succeeded in establishing sexual equality may be determined by analyzing contemporary female political activity, their successful reforms, their opposition, the emergence of militant feminism, the legacy of the French Revolution, and comparable movements in other revolutions. This analysis would suggest that protofeminist movements during the French Revolution did not succeed in establishing sexual equality at the time, however, it facilitated the emergence and the future development of feminism.

The establishment of sexual equality was a failure because of the lack of organisation in female political activity and a division of the social classes. Primarily, women's rights activists failed to gain the support of the public and of the leading revolutionaries during the Revolution. One reason for this was the lack of organizational experience, as illustrated by the development of political clubs independent of one another and the isolation of political activists.[4] As a result of the failure in the organisation of female political activism, support could not be gained and sexual equality could not be established. Additionally, the presence of the traditional division of social classes, as pictured in A. P.'s political cartoon, hindered the establishment of sexual egalitarianism.[5] While the feminist aspirations of the women of the bourgeoisie revolved around the preservation of their newly acquired social position, the women of the working class were

---

[3] (Taylor 1999, p. 264)
[4] (Abray, 1975, p. 61)
[5] *Source 1* (The British Museum, 2019)

more concerned with general political rights.[6] The bourgeoisie expressed interest in questions of legal status, divorce, and education. These were secondary issues to the working class, which instead was focused on hunger, unemployment, and inflation. The political club *The Society of Revolutionary Women* (the *Républicaines*) represented the interests of women of the working class.[7] Although the club did not emphasize explicit feminist demands, it recognized that the establishment of general workers' rigths was dependent on feminine rights, and therefore expressed sympathy for women's emancipation.[8] The division between the women of the working class and the women of the bourgeoisie agitated the disorganized nature of female political activity. Collaboration between the protofeminist movements would not be possible considering their widely differing aims. Therefore, the lack of organizational experience coupled with the traditional division of the classes meant that the establishment of sexual equality was predestined to fail.

Simultaneously, female political activity during the Revolution was somewhat successful in establishing sexual equality through limited educational and marital reforms. The opening of a *lycée* to women in 1786 was a stepping stone for the recognition of female intellectual equality. Made possible by the activists Roland and Condorcet, "the *National Assembly* decided to allow girls to attend school until 8 years of age".[9] Although the educational reform had a limited effect on the relationship between men and women in contemporary France, the admission of female education was a significant advancement towards the future establishment of sexual equality. At

---

[6] (Hufton, 1992, p. 10)
[7] (Racz, 1952, p. 161-168)
[8] (Abray, 1975, p. 52)
[9] (Bessiéres & Niedzwiecki, 1991, p. 11)

the same time, there were advancements within marital egalitarianism, as a legislation giving women "the right of divorce" was passed in 1792.[10] "Divorce on the grounds of incompatibility, mutual consent and if one of the spouses was abandoned for more than two years" became legal. [11] As this right enabled women significant freedom, it could be argued that from 1792, they "acquired the dignity of free persons".[12] This newfound freedom would indicate a success in the establishment of sexual equality, however, exclusively with reference to marriage. Therefore, the establishment of equality of the sexes was only partially successful because of the introduction of limited educational and marital reforms.

The governmental suppression of organized female political activity contributed to the failure of the protofeminist movements to establish sexual equality. Soon after the establishment of the *Républicaines*, the club "gained the unfavorable attention of the *National Convention*", which voted on October 30 1793 to ban all female political clubs.[13] Thus were not only female political rights rejected, but even the "right to engage in any form of organized politics" was denied.[14] Although female political activity was restricted, women continued with their charitable efforts, yet only passively. The suppressive effect of the ban of organized female political activity was exacerbated by the imprisonment and execution of political activists, such as Olympe de Gouges. [15] As a result of her publications, including the *Declaration of the Rights of Woman*[16], de Gouges

---

[10] (Diamond, 1990, p. 101)
[11] (Bessiéres & Niedzwiecki, 1991, p. 18)
[12] (Bessiéres & Niedzwiecki, 1991, p. 18)
[13] (Hunt, 1996, p. 28)
[14] (Hunt, 1996, p. 29)
[15] (Hunt, 1996, p. 27)
[16] *Source 2* (Bessiéres & Niedzwiecki, 1991, p. 14-16)

was executed in 1793 for "attempting to pervert the republic with her writings".[17] The fear of a similar fate caused a strong disinclination among women to engage in political activity, or even advocate for sexual equality. In other words, the suppression of organized female political activity contributed to the failure of the establishment of equality of the sexes.

The establishment of sexual equality was somewhat of a success because it led to the emergence of militant feminism. An example of a situation in which women would fight "alongside the armies" was the *Women's March on Versailles*.[18] Although the invasion of the King's palace was not explicitly feminist in nature, female militancy generally had feminist overtones.[19] The emancipation of women would be meaningless unless the issue of famine was resolved first. In other words, the emergence of feminist aspirations in the working class was reflected in "general plebian aims".[20] This was in turn expressed through the aforementioned political clubs.[21] Additionally, the *Républicaines* advocated "for the establishment of armed military groups of women".[22] Regardless of the threat of international and civil war, the appeals of the *Républicaines* were rejected.[23] In addition to women being excluded from political militancy, there was limited time for women to partake in "revolutionary combat", as a result of the absence of their husbands.[24] At the same time, however, this male absence meant that women had to adopt a more significant economic and social role in their place.[25] While it could be argued that

---

[17] (Bessiéres & Niedzwiecki, 1991, p. 16)
[18] (Bessiéres & Niedzwiecki, 1991, p. 20)
[19] (Encyclopaedia Britannica, 2019)
[20] (Racz, 1952, p. 160)
[21] (Racz, 1952, p. 160)
[22] (Hunt, 1996, p. 28)
[23] (Hunt, 1996, p. 28)
[24] (Bessiéres & Niedzwiecki, 1991, p. 19)
[25] (Bessiéres & Niedzwiecki, 1991, p. 19)

this new family dynamic contributed to the development of sexual equality, it was not

necessarily caused by the protofeminist movements, but rather by the Revolution itself. Still, the

emergence of militant feminism during the Revolution contributed to some, although limited,

form of sexual equality.

The legacy of the protofeminist movements and the consideration of perspectives contribute to

their partial success in establishing sexual equality. Although the French Revolution did not

seem to produce significant results for sexual equality in contemporary France, the development

of feminism continued in several European countries, including England and Germany.[26]

Additionally, it could be argued that the protofeminist movements of the French Revolution were

successful in establishing sexual equality in comparison to other political movements of the

eighteenth century. For instance, in the American and Dutch revolutions, women would form

clubs, however, not for explicit political purposes as in France. It was only in France during the

French Revolution that demands for sexual egalitarianism were made. The publicly expressed

demands for women's rights in the French Revolution facilitated the future development of

sexual equality.[27] Therefore, because the protofeminist movements of the French Revolution

enabled the development of women's rights, more than any other comparable movements, the

establishment of sexual equality can be considered partially successful.

In conclusion, the failures of the protofeminist movements during the French Revolution

overshadowed their successes. While reforms were made within marriage and education, the

---

[26] (Bessiéres & Niedzwiecki, 1991, p. 11)
[27] (Hunt, 1996, p. 29)

extent of the reforms did not make women anywhere near equal to men. The extent of the

governmental suppression of female political activity became clear through the silencing of

political activists. Militant feminism did emerge, causing a shift in the roles of women, however,

it was not of a strictly feminist nature. Despite the advancements within feminism that the

movements of the Revolution enabled in the future, they did not succeed in establishing equality

of the sexes in their own time.

Section 3: Reflection

The historical investigation of the extent to which protofeminist movements of the French Revolution succeeded in establishing sexual equality has illustrated the implications of certain historical methods to me. The methods that struck me in particular were the ones relating to the use of different perspectives and the interpretation of sources. Firstly, the use of differing perspectives in a historical investigation can aid in ensuring that the sources themselves are objective, while also balancing one's own judgement of the past. The effect of this on my investigation was the consideration of historical movements with similar political contexts. Effectively, on the one hand, the establishment of sexual equality in the French Revolution can be seen as a failure. On the other hand, the extent to which the protofeminst movements succeeded in establishing sexual equality was much more significant in the French Revolution than that of the American and Dutch revolutions. In other words, the question of the success of the protofeminist movements is dependent on the perspective from which it is answered. Moreover, the role of interpretation in historical investigations enabled me to determine the values and limitations of the primary sources I evaluated in detail. The exploration of interpretation as a historical method led to my appreciation of its advantages and disadvantages. Interpretation occurs within the sources themselves, as well as in the mind of the historian. Therefore, I attempted to be cautious of leaving too much up for interpretation as it would have hindered me from arguing a reasoned, objective conclusion.

Additionally, the investigation has caused me to recognize the challenge facing historians concerning the definition of concepts. For instance, throughout my research I discovered that some sources disagreed on the definition of feminism. While certain sources viewed the history of feminism and the history of women as common to one another, others explicitly pointed out that they should be separate. The sources of the latter group, particularly the ones concerning militant feminism, underlined that feminism as we know it did not exist at all during the French Revolution. Because of the constant change in meanings behind concepts, modern definitions can not always be applied to the past without implications. This ties in with the limitations of interpretation. The interpretation of concepts by individual historians poses a risk of them distorting the past with personal opinion.

BIBLIOGRAPHY + APPENDICES OMITTED

3. EXAMPLE THREE (24/25)

Name: 'Was the 30th of September Movement instigated by the PKI (Communist Party of Indonesia) or officials within the Army?'

Author: Anonymous

Session: November 2020

Level: HL

Table of Contents

Section 1: Identification & Evaluation of sources

This investigation will explore the question: **Was the 30th September Movement instigated by the PKI (Communist Party of Indonesia) or officials within the Army?**

The sources to be evaluated are Brigadier General Supardjo's analysis "*Some factors that influenced the defeat of the "September 30th Movement" as viewed from a Military Perspective*",[1] written in 1966 and Benedict R. Anderson and Ruth T. McVey's book "*A Preliminary Analysis of the October 1, 1965 Coup in Indonesia*",[2] published in 1971. The two sources are relevant since the first suggests that the PKI was directly involved while the second source suggests the movement was purely an internal army affair.[3]

The first source is valuable based on its origin. The author, Brigadier General Supardjo, was a conspirator present at Halim Air Base[4] on the day of the movement and had written his analysis for colleagues before his arrest[5] on January 12, 1967,[6] providing a valuable first-hand account. The purpose of the document is also valuable since as a post-mortem analysis, it reveals all the participants of the coup, showing the PKI's complicity in the affair.[7] Its content is also valuable since it asserts PKI involvement and

---

[1] Brigadier General Supardjo, "Some Factors That Influenced the Defeat of "the September 30th Movement" as Viewed from a Military Perspective, Jakarta, 1966," in *Pretext for Mass Murder: The September 30th Movement and Suharto's Coup d'état in Indonesia,* ed. John Roosa (Madison, Wisconsin: University of Wisconsin Press, 2006), 227.

[2] Benedict R. O'G. Anderson and Ruth T. McVey, *A Preliminary Analysis of the October 1, 1965 Coup in Indonesia* (Singapore: Equinox Publishing, 2009), 1.

[3] Anderson and Ruth T. McVey, *A Preliminary Analysis,* 60.

[4] Halim Air Base was the hideout for the core organisers of the movement

[5] John Roosa, *Pretext for Mass Murder: The September 30th Movement and Suharto's Coup d'etat in Indonesia* (Madison, Wisconsin: The University of Wisconsin Press, 2006), 82-83.

[6] Guy J. Pauker, "Indonesia: The Year of Transition," *Asian Survey* 7, no. 2 (February 1967): 146, under "A Survey of Asia in 1966: Part II," http://www.jstor.org/stable/2642526 (accessed October 22, 2019).

[7] Roosa, *Pretext for Mass Murder,* 83-87.

leadership through explicit statements like "an operation that was led directly by the party".[8]

However, the source is limited based on its origin. Supardjo was not a core organiser, serving a more supplementary role.[9] His unfamiliarity with the initial planning stages could have thus hindered his analysis.[10] In addition, its purpose is limited as Supardjo intended his document to explain tactical errors made by coup leaders rather than seek out those responsible for it. The document's contents are also limited by its omission of details regarding the initial planning stages.[11] In Supardjo's own words, "compared to the length of time of all the preparations, the time of my involvement was very brief"[12] and records only what he could witness, the day of the coup and the days directly before and after.[13]

The second source is valuable based on origin since both Anderson and McVey were graduate students from Cornell University studying Indonesia when they wrote their paper in 1966.[14] Anderson was a political scientist and professor of international studies[15] and thus has the proper credentials and academic appointment. The source is also valuable in purpose since it intends to present an alternate view of the coup being an

---

[8] Supardjo, "Some Factors," 241.
[9] Roosa, Pretext for Mass Murder, 86.
[10] Ibid., 83.
[11] Ibid.
[12] Supardjo, "Some Factors," 228.
[13] Ibid.
[14] Sewell Chan, "Benedict Anderson, Scholar Who Saw Nations as 'Imagined,' Dies at 79," The New York Times, December 14, 2015, https://www.nytimes.com/2015/12/15/world/asia/benedict-anderson-scholar-who-saw-nations-as-imagined-dies-at-79.html (accessed May 20, 2019).
[15] Patricio Abinales, "Yes, Benedict Anderson was a political scientist," The Washington Post, December 21, 2015, https://www.washingtonpost.com/news/monkey-cage/wp/2015/12/21/yes-benedict-anderson-was-a-political-scientist/?noredirect=on&utm_term=.89620c32fa8a (accessed May 20, 2019).

internal army affair by focusing on the political volatility and complexity of the Indonesian military.[16] It is valuable content wise since it is based on contemporary transcripts made by the movement, who themselves asserted that it was entirely an affair within the military.[17]

However, the source is limited in origin since it was first produced in 1966 and subsequently published in full in 1971. Since then, other documents have been discovered like the aforementioned Supardjo document, meaning the writers did not have the benefit of hindsight to consider multiple perspectives from an assortment of historical documents. The source is also limited by its content since it omits key circumstantial evidence, like the PKI's steadily heightening militancy and accelerating drive to power prior to the coup, [18] to depict the PKI as the victim of a coup caused by the army.

528 words

---

[16] Anderson and Ruth T. McVey, *A Preliminary Analysis*, 10.
[17] Ibid., 167-209.
[18] Justus M. van der Kroef, "Interpretations of the 1965 Indonesian Coup: A Review of the Literature," *Pacific Affairs* 43, no. 4 (1970-1971): 563, https://www.jstor.org/stable/2754905?seq=7#metadata_info_tab_contents (accessed May 26, 2019).

Section 2: Investigation

On 30 September 1965, a group of Indonesian military officers led by Lieutenant Colonel Untung, battalion commander of then President Sukarno's bodyguard, kidnapped and killed six of Indonesia's top military leaders.[19] Seizing control of the Radio Republik Indonesia[20] in Jakarta, Untung himself proclaimed the movement was "directed against generals who were members of the self-styled Council of Generals",[21] and to "prevent such a counter-revolutionary coup (by the Council of Generals)".[22] The 30th September movement thus presented itself as a counter coup with troops loyal to Sukarno.[23] However the movement failed due to poor planning and logistical issues[24], causing KOSTRAD[25] Director General Suharto took over army leadership and convinced battalions supporting the coup to abort their mission.[26] In the months that followed, Suharto and his associates rose to political ascendancy by blaming the PKI as masterminds of the movement, triggering a politicide leading to the deaths of around 1 million and the complete destruction of the PKI.[27] Debating views about the PKI's complicity in the affair have since risen with Supardjo claiming that it was an "operation led directly by the party"[28] while historians Benedict R. Anderson and Ruth T. McVey have posited the movement as purely an internal army affair with officers attempting to use PKI

---

[19] Audrey Kahnin, *Historical Dictionary of Indonesia* (Maryland: Rowman & Littlefield, 2015), 170.
[20] The national radio station of Indonesia
[21] Initial Statement of Lieutenant Colonel Untung, Jakarta, October 1, 1965, in *Selected Documents Relating to the "September 30th Movement" and Its Epilogue*, ed. Cornell University Press; Southeast Asia Program Publications at Cornell University, *Indonesia*, no. 1 (1966): 134-135.
[22] Ibid.
[23] Roosa, *Pretext for Mass Murder*, 3.
[24] Supardjo, "Some Factors," 231-237.
[25] Army Strategic Reserve Command, a formation of the Indonesian Army
[26] John Hughes, *The End of Sukarno: A Coup that misfired: A purge that ran wild* (Singapore: Archipelago Press, 2002), 74.
[27] Adrian Vickers, *A History of Modern Indonesia* (New York: Cambridge University Press, 2013), 164.
[28] Supardjo, "Some Factors," 241.

leadership and Sukarno for their own benefit.[29] Although the movement was supported by PKI members like Kamaruzaman Sjam who led the communist wing of the movement,[30] the PKI as a whole did not entirely instigate the coup; instead it was instigated by certain PKI leaders and the army.[31]

Firstly, evidence of PKI instigation can be seen in the Supardjo document whereby Supardjo states the movement's original plan was for it to "progress in stages and then suddenly change into a purely PKI movement".[32] Supardjo identifies the movement's leadership as being divided into three groups, consisting of "the Head Group, the Sjam and friends group and the Untung and friends group".[33] Kamaruzaman Sjam identified himself in his testimony at the 1967 Mahmilub[34] trials as the "leader of the PKI's Special Bureau"[35] who "received orders directly from the head of the party".[36] This is coupled with the Indonesian Army's narrative, that the PKI was indeed responsible since General Secretary of the PKI, D. N. Aidit, was present at Halim Air Base, where the movement had held President Sukarno.[37] Further evidence was indicated by the fact that volunteers from PKI organizations like *Pemuda Rakyat*[38] were part of sub-units responsible for abducting and killing the generals.[39] The PKI also sought to have a hand in the movement

---

[29] Anderson and Ruth T. McVey, *A Preliminary Analysis*, 10.
[30] Roosa, *Pretext for Mass Murder*, 203.
[31] Ibid.
[32] Supardjo, "Some Factors," 241.
[33] Ibid., 233.
[34] Extraordinary Military Tribunal, a court set up by Suharto to process the movement's members
[35] The Testimony of Sjam, Jakarta, 1967, in *Pretext for Mass Murder: The September 30th Movement and Suharto's Coup d'état* in Indonesia, ed. John Roosa (Madison, Wisconsin: University of Wisconsin Press, 2006), 245-247.
[36] Ibid.
[37] Nugroho Notosusanto and Ismail Saleh, *The coup attempt of the September 30 Movement in Indonesia* (Jakarta: P.T. Pembimbing Masa-Jakarta, 1968), 38.
[38] Youth wing of the PKI
[39] Ibid., 20-21.

owing to Sukarno's frail health. Sukarno's health was long a matter of political concern[40] and the PKI feared an open break between him and the army would put it in a position where it was virtually defenseless.[41] Thus, due to PKI leadership and the fear of Sukarno's death leading to its vulnerability, the PKI thus masterminded the affair as a pre-emptive measure to secure its interests.

Furthermore, the PKI's heavy involvement can be implied by its actions before and after the coup. Beforehand, the PKI had operated a network of 700 "progressive officers'' within the four branches of the armed services, through Sjam's activities.[42] Around 3000 people were also trained by the PKI in anticipation for the movement[43] at Lubang Buaya.[44] Even D. N. Aidit discussed the possibility of a coup during meetings of the Politburo of the PKI Central Committee, sending out cadres to different provinces and instructing them to "listen to the announcements over the Central RRI and support the Revolutionary Council".[45] On October 2, the *Harian Rakjat* published a cartoon depicting a "Council of Generals" figure propped up by the Central Intelligence Agency (CIA) punched in the face by the 30th September Movement, showing its open support for the movement.[46] Another consideration was Sukarno's open support for the PKI, who introduced his signature

---

[40] J. D. Legge, *Sukarno: A Political Biography* (Singapore: Archipelago Press, 2003), 430.

[41] Harold Crouch, *The Army and Politics in Indonesia* (Singapore: Equinox Publishing, 2007), 82.

[42] Victor M. Fic, *Anatomy of the Jakarta Coup: October 1, 1965* (Jakarta: Yayasan Obor Indonesia, 2005), 9.

[43] Nugroho Notosusanto, *30 years of Indonesia's Independence* (Jakarta: State Secretariat of the Republic of Indonesia, 1975), 520.

[44] A suburb of Jakarta, where the bodies of the killed generals were dumped

[45] Sudisman, "Analysis of responsibility: Defence speech of SUDISMAN General Secretary of the Indonesian Communist Party at his trial before the Special Military Tribunal, Jakarta, 21 July,1967." Digital Image, https://www.marxists.org/history/indonesia/Sudisman%20%281967%29%20-%20Analysis%20of%20Responsibility.pdf. Translated by B. R. O'G. Anderson. Extracted from https://www.marxists.org.

[46] Harian Rakjat, "An editorial cartoon from the front page of the Communist Party of Indonesia (PKI) newspaper "Harian Rakyat" published 2 October 1965," Digital Image, https://commons.wikimedia.org/wiki/File:HarianRakjat2Oct1965.jpg, extracted from Wikimedia commons.

policy of Nasakom in 1957, balancing Nationalism-Regionalism and Communism.[47] Sukarno himself was determined to purge top army officials whom he saw opposing him for his vision of seeing Indonesia being closely aligned with the People's Republic of China,[48] sharing this same goal with the PKI.[49] In early 1965, China encouraged Sukarno to establish the Fifth Force, a militia group of armed peasants and workers, helping the PKI gain an edge on its rivals like the army.[50] Chinese arms were supplied to workers and farmers who were a core force of the PKI and carried out the movement in other parts of the country.[51] Therefore, the PKI's dubious actions near the coup date, coupled with evidence of both Sukarno's and foreign support, renders the PKI responsible for the coup's development.

However, as Benedict Anderson and Ruth McVey argue, the PKI was not responsible since the internal army dynamics was crucial for causing the coup. Within the Diponegoro division which executed the coup, there was discontent, possibly explaining why the movement took root mainly in Central Java where the division's military infrastructure was located.[52] Strong cultural clashes within the military played a huge role, with members of the Diponegoro being deeply rooted in traditional conservative Javanese culture in contrast to senior officers like General Ahmed Yani[53] who belonged to the liberal, modernised Jakarta metropolitan elite.[54] Hatred for Yani and his social class

---

[47] Aco Manafe, *Terperpu: Reveals PKI's Betrayal in 1965 and the trial of the perpetrators* (Jakarta: Pustaka Sinar Harapan, 2008), 6.

[48] Fic, *Anatomy of the Jakarta Coup*, 5.

[49] Sukarno and the so-called Untung-putsch: eye-witness report by Bambang S. Widjanarko, 1974, *in The Devious Dalang*, ed. Rahadi S. Karni (The Hague: Interdoc Publishing House, 1974), 47.

[50] Taomo Zhou, "China and the Thirtieth of September Movement," Indonesia, no. 98 (October 2014): 31-34, http://www.jstor.org/stable/10.5728/indonesia.98.0029 (accessed October 23, 2019).

[51] Ibid., 83-86.

[52] Crouch, *The Army and Politics in Indonesia*, 113-114.

[53] Commander of the Army, one of the military leaders killed by the movement

[54] Anderson and Ruth T. McVey, *A Preliminary Analysis*, 18-20.

would also explain why after killing him, the coup executors wiped out the Yani faction among top generals.[55] Further discontent was also caused by resentment of lower level officers towards tough promotional opportunity, corruption among generals and the delay of sending army troops to the disputed Kalimantan region.[56] Coup members also sought to initiate a "return to the spirit of Jogja",[57] reviving the Indonesian Revolutionary spirit by establishing the Indonesian Revolution Council.[58] Therefore, the coup was started by revolutionary army officials who wanted to purge the army of libertarian elements, reinforcing the PKI's innocence.

Furthermore, the PKI's innocence can also be proven as organising such an unanticipated violent movement was not its modus operandi.[59] The PKI was a well organised party that was integrated into the system under Sukarno's Guided democracy.[60] Moreover, the army view that the PKI was culpable based on party leader Aidit's presence at Halim Air Base is flawed since Aidit was never brought to public trial to explain his actions, instead executed beforehand.[61] The myth of China's involvement in the coup can also be dispelled. Although the Chinese were sympathetic to the cause of the coup, specific details of coup planning would unlikely be divulged owing to the secrecy of the operation.[62] Thus, due to the ambiguity of evidence for the PKI's

---

[55] M. C. Ricklefs, *A History of Modern Indonesia since c.1200* (Hampshire: Palgrave Macmillan, 2008), 319.
[56] Anderson and Ruth T. McVey, *A Preliminary Analysis*, 23.
[57] Ibid., 23.
[58] Decree No. 1 on the Establishment of the Indonesian Revolution Council, Jakarta, October 1, 1965, in *Selected Documents Relating to the "September 30th Movement " and its Epilogue*, ed. Cornell University Press; Southeast Asia Program Publications at Cornell University, *Indonesia*, no. 1 (1966): 136.
[59] Roosa, *Pretext for Mass Murder*, 5.
[60] Kahnin, *Historical Dictionary of Indonesia*, 178.
[61] Arif Zulkifli and Bagja Hidayat, Aidit*: Two Faces of Dipa Nusantara* (Jakarta: Gramedia Popular Library, 2010), 77.
[62] Helen-Louise Hunter, *Sukarno and the Indonesian Coup: The Untold Story* (Westport, Conn: Praeger, 2007), 180-181.

involvement, the case is not clear enough to place total responsibility of the coup on the shoulders of the PKI, reinforcing their innocence.

Despite the lack of direct documentation, some PKI leaders such as Sjam and Aidit did act beyond their mandates and collaborated with Army officials to instigate the coup.[63] They singled out key Army generals to attack, portraying them as corrupt, oppressive and possibly in league with the CIA.[64] However, while the trials of Sjam at Mahmilub show a degree of PKI responsibility, they were show trials conducted with the intent to implicate the PKI,[65] meaning the responsibility accorded to the PKI could have been exaggerated. Those tried were often tortured beforehand.[66] Furthermore, during the movement, local cadres in Central Java were thoroughly confused and claimed a lack of foreknowledge of the coup,[67] showing it was not an initiative planned solely by the party. Newly declassified CIA documents have also shown that the Army had anticipated such a movement with American help[68] and intended to "exploit its (the movement) opportunity to move against

---

[63] Olle Tornquist, review of *Pretext for Mass Murder: The September 30th Movement and Suharto's Coup d'état in Indonesia,* by John Roosa, *International Review of Social History* 52, no. 2 (2007): 310.
[64] Leslie Palmier, "The 30 September Movement in Indonesia," *Modern Asian Studies* 5, no. 1 (1971): 1, http://www.jstor.org/stable/311652 (accessed November 16, 2019).
[65] Geoffrey B. Robinson, *The Killing Season: A History of the Indonesian Massacres, 1965-1966* (Princeton, New Jersey: Princeton University Press, 2018), 63.
[66] Ibid., 69.
[67] Marshall Green, 5th Ambassador, American Embassy in Jakarta to Secretary of State, Foreign Service of the United States of America, Nov 20, 1965, Telegram 971, RG 84, Entry P 339, Jakarta Embassy Files, Box 14, Folder 6 pol 23-9, National Security Archives, https://nsarchive2.gwu.edu//dc.html?doc=4107014-Document-04-US-Embassy-in-Jakarta-Telegram-971 (accessed November 16, 2019).
[68] Geoffrey Robinson, *The Dark Side of Paradise: Political Violence in Bali* (Ithaca: Cornell University Press, 1995), 283.

the PKI."[69] This undermines the Army's view of the PKI being the sole instigator, implicating that it was using the movement as a pretext to eliminate the PKI instead.[70]

In conclusion, the movement was neither instigated by the PKI or army officials alone, instead it was a collaboration by certain members within PKI leadership and dissident army officials. It was thus instigated as a pre-emptive strike against right-wing high command.[71]

1328 words

---

[69] The Indonesian Situation (Report #14 as of 11:00 A.M. EDT), CIA Report no. 14 to White House, Central Intelligence Agency, Office of Current Intelligence, October 5, 1965, CIA-RDP79T00472A001500040014-7, Freedom of Information Act Electronic Reading Room, https://www.cia.gov/library/readingroom/docs/CIA-RDP79T00472A001500040014-7.pdf (accessed November 17, 2019).
[70] Roosa, *Pretext for Mass Murder*, 31.
[71] Ibid., 203.

Section 3: Reflection

The first challenge that I faced and shared with historians was evaluating conflicting interpretations. Anderson and McVey assert the movement being a purely internal army affair[72] while the historians Notosusanto and Saleh believe it was masterminded by the PKI.[73] To solve the problem, I consulted recent scholarship, such as Roosa's *Pretext for Mass Murder* that presented new interpretations and a synthesis of views, suggesting it was a collaborative effort and the Army had anticipated such a movement.[74] To gain more perspectives, I consulted different primary sources such as court trials, speeches and even a cartoon that reflects contemporary views by movement's members. Gathering different sources highlighted to me the importance for historians to use a variety of sources to ensure greater reliability.

Another challenge I faced was the selective omission and historical negationism by some Indonesian historians to fit the stance of Suharto's New Order. For instance, Notosusanto and Saleh had relied primarily on confessions by Sjam in a staged trial that were never convincingly proven to Western academics.[75] Such works were often polemical and often played up the viciousness of the PKI killings while failing to mention the massive post movement killings resulting in around a million dead.[76] I overcame this by using works by authors like Roosa who had consulted other significant evidence like Supardjo's document, the only document written by a coup participant before Supardjo's

[72] Anderson and Ruth T. McVey, *A Preliminary Analysis*, 10.
[73] Notosusanto and Saleh, *The coup attempt*, 150.
[74] Roosa, *Pretext for Mass Murder*, 224.
[75] Hamish McDonald, "Puppetmaster's ambition knew no end," The Sydney Morning Herald, January 28, 2008, https://www.smh.com.au/world/puppetmasters-ambition-knew-no-end-20080128-gdrym7.html. (accessed November 21, 2019).
[76] Ibid.

arrest.[77] This made me learn the importance for historians to determine the veracity of their sources and the circumstances under which they were made.

I was also faced with the issue of censorship, a problem faced by other historians. In trying to find out if Suharto's faction had any role in the movement that would severely undermine their credibility as the "saviours" of the nation, I learned that Suharto's government had heavily suppressed discussions and documents relating to the incident.[78] I circumvented this by accessing newly declassified documents from US archives and found clear evidence of Suharto's faction colluding with the CIA to pre-empt the coup so Suharto could seize power, thus severely undermining their credibility.

344 words

Total: 2200 words

---

[77] Roosa, *Pretext for Mass Murder*, 83.
[78] Vannessa Hearman, "Indonesians should be able to talk about 1965 massacres without fear of censorship," The Conversation, October 26, 2015, http://theconversation.com/indonesians-should-be-able-to-talk-about-1965-massacres-without-fear-of-censorship-49729. (accessed February 2, 2020).

Bibliography

Books

Anderson, Benedict R. O'G. and Ruth Thomas McVey. *A Preliminary Analysis of the October 1, 1965 Coup in Indonesia*. Singapore: Equinox Publishing, 2009.

B. Robinson, Geoffrey. *The Killing Season: A History of the Indonesian Massacres, 1965-1966*. Princeton, New Jersey: Princeton University Press, 2018.

Crouch, Harold. *The Army and Politics in Indonesia*. Singapore: Equinox Publishing, 2007.

Hunter, Helen-Louise. *Sukarno and the Indonesian Coup: The Untold Story*. Westport, Conn: Praeger, 2007.

Hughes, John. *The End of Sukarno - A Coup that misfired: A purge that ran wild*. Singapore: Archipelago Press, 2002.

Kahnin, Audrey. *Historical Dictionary of Indonesia*. Maryland: Rowman & Littlefield, 2015.

Legge, J. D. *Sukarno: A Political Biography*. Singapore: Archipelago Press, 2003.

Manafe, Aco. *Terperpu: Reveals PKI's Betrayal in 1965 and the trial of the perpetrators*. Jakarta: Pustaka Sinar Harapan, 2008.

M. Fic, Victor. *Anatomy of the Jakarta Coup: October 1, 1965*. Jakarta: Yayasan Obor Indonesia, 2005.

Notosusanto, Nugroho. and Ismail Saleh. *The coup attempt of the September 30 Movement in Indonesia*. Jakarta: P.T. Pembimbing Masa-Jakarta, 1968.

Notosusanto, Nugroho. *30 years of Indonesia's Independence*. Jakarta: State Secretariat of the Republic of Indonesia, 1975.

Robinson, Geoffrey. *The Dark Side of Paradise: Political Violence in Bali*. Ithaca: Cornell University Press, 1995.

Roosa, John. *Pretext for Mass Murder: The September 30th Movement and Suharto's Coup d'etat in Indonesia*. Madison, Wisconsin: University of Wisconsin Press, 2006.

Ricklefs, M. C. *A History of Modern Indonesia since c.1200*. Hampshire: Palgrave Macmillan, 2008.

Vickers, Adrian. *A History of Modern Indonesia*. New York: Cambridge University Press, 2013.

Zulkifli, Arif. and Bagja Hidayat. *Aidit: Two Faces of Dipa Nusantara*. Jakarta: Gramedia Popular Library, 2010.

Book Reviews

Tornquist, Olle. Review of Pretext for Mass Murder: The September 30th Movement and Suharto's Coup d'état in Indonesia, by John Roosa. *International Review of Social History* 52, no. 2 (2007): 308-311.

Newspaper Articles

Abinales, Patricio. "Yes, Benedict Anderson was a political scientist." *The Washington Post*. December 21, 2015. https://www.washingtonpost.com/news/monkey-cage/wp/2015/12/21/yes-benedict-anderson-was-a-political-scientist/?noredirect=on&utm_term=.89620c32fa8a (accessed May 20, 2019).

Chan, Sewell. "Benedict Anderson, Scholar Who Saw Nations as 'Imagined,' Dies at 79." *The New York Times*. December 14, 2015. https://www.nytimes.com/2015/12/15/world/asia/benedict-anderson-scholar-who-saw-nations-as-imagined-dies-at-79.html (accessed May 20, 2019).

Hearman, Vannessa. "Indonesians should be able to talk about 1965 massacres without fear of censorship." The Conversation. October 26, 2015. http://theconversation.com/indonesians-should-be-able-to-talk-about-1965-massacres-without-fear-of-censorship-49729 (accessed February 2, 2020).

McDonald, Hamish. "Puppetmaster's ambition knew no end." The Sydney Morning Herald. January 28, 2008. https://www.smh.com.au/world/puppetmasters-ambition-knew-no-end-20080128-gdrym7.html (accessed November 21, 2019).

Primary Sources

Brigadier General Supardjo, Some Factors That Influenced the Defeat of "the September 30th Movement" as Viewed from a Military Perspective, Jakarta, 1966, in *Pretext for Mass Murder: The September 30th Movement and Suharto's Coup d'état in Indonesia*, ed. John Roosa (Madison, Wisconsin: University of Wisconsin Press, 2006).

Decree No. 1 on the Establishment of the Indonesian Revolution Council, Jakarta, October 1, 1965, in *Selected Documents Relating to the "September 30th Movement" and its Epilogue,* ed. Cornell University Press; Southeast Asia Program Publications at Cornell University, *Indonesia,* no. 1 (1966).

Green, Marshall. 5th Ambassador, American Embassy in Jakarta to Secretary of State, Foreign Service of the United States of America, Nov 20, 1965, Telegram 971, RG 84, Entry P 339, Jakarta Embassy Files, Box 14, Folder 6 pol 23-9, National Security Archives. https://nsarchive2.gwu.edu//dc.html?doc=4107014-Document-04-US-Embassy-in-Jakarta-Telegram-971 (accessed November 16, 2019).

Initial Statement of Lieutenant Colonel Untung, Jakarta, October 1, 1965, in *Selected Documents Relating to the "September 30th Movement" and Its Epilogue,* ed. Cornell University Press; Southeast Asia Program Publications at Cornell University, *Indonesia,* no. 1 (1966).

Rakjat, Harian. "An editorial cartoon from the front page of the Communist Party of Indonesia (PKI) newspaper "Harian Rakyat" published 2 October 1965." Digital Image. https://commons.wikimedia.org/wiki/File:HarianRakjat2Oct1965.jpg. Extracted from Wikimedia commons.

Sudisman, "Analysis of responsibility: Defence speech of SUDISMAN General Secretary of the Indonesian Communist Party at his trial before the Special Military Tribunal, Jakarta, 21 July,1967." Digital Image. https://www.marxists.org/history/indonesia/Sudisman%20%281967%29%20-%20Analysis%20of%20Responsibility.pdf. Translated by B. R. O'G. Anderson. Extracted from https://www.marxists.org.

Sukarno and the so-called Untung-putsch: eye-witness report by Bambang S. Widjanarko, 1974, *in The Devious Dalang,* ed. Rahadi S. Karni (The Hague: Interdoc Publishing House, 1974).

The Indonesian Situation (Report #14 as of 11:00 A.M. EDT), CIA Report no. 14 to White House, Central Intelligence Agency, Office of Current Intelligence, October 5, 1965, CIA-RDP79T00472A001500040014-7, Freedom of Information Act Electronic Reading Room. https://www.cia.gov/library/readingroom/docs/CIA-RDP79T00472A001500040014-7.pdf (accessed November 17, 2019).

The Testimony of Sjam, Jakarta, 1967, in Pretext for Mass Murder: The September 30th Movement and Suharto's Coup d'état in Indonesia, ed. John Roosa (Madison, Wisconsin: University of Wisconsin Press, 2006).

Scholarly Journals

Palmier, Leslie. "The 30 September Movement in Indonesia." *Modern Asian Studies* 5, no. 1 (1971): 1-20. http://www.jstor.org/stable/311652 (accessed November 16, 2019).

Pauker, Guy J. "Indonesia: The Year of Transition." *Asian Survey* 7, no. 2 (February 1967): 146. http://www.jstor.org/stable/2642526 (accessed October 22, 2019).

van der Kroef, Justus M. "Interpretations of the 1965 Indonesian Coup: A Review of the Literature." *Pacific Affairs* 43, no. 4 (1970-1971): 563. https://www.jstor.org/stable/2754905?seq=7#metadata_info_tab_contents (accessed May 26, 2019).

Zhou, Taomo. "China and the Thirtieth of September Movement." *Indonesia*, no. 98 (October 2014): 31-34. http://www.jstor.org/stable/10.5728/indonesia.98.0029 (accessed October 23, 2019).

4. EXAMPLE FOUR (22/25)

Name: 'To What Extent did the Industrialization of Penicillin Affect the Mortality Rate of Ill Allied Soldiers During World War II?

Author: Anonymous

Session: May 2019

Level: HL

Section I

Penicillin was introduced in the late 1920s after its effects were discovered by professor Alexander Fleming. Even today, antibiotics play a large role in the maintenance of human health. However, the immediate effects of these drugs seem to hold greater significance during the 20th century, especially during the World War II era; some historians even argue that the introduction of penicillin played a direct role in the Allies' victory. However, the degree of this claim's factuality remains unclear. And so, the question persists: To what extent did the industrialization of penicillin affect the mortality rate of ill Allied soldiers during World War II?

The first examined source is a *New York Times* newspaper article titled "Penicillin Shown to Cure Syphilis" published on December 16, 1949. The author is unknown. Still, the article is valuable because it was published by a reliable source. Although it is a secondary source, its close timing with WWII provides a valuable perspective into the happenings of the 20th century (in contrast to an article written in the present day). Conversely, the same piece of the origin pose limitations; because it was written in 1949, the analysis of the medicine's effects on the war may not be complete. Furthermore, the document is written from a journalist's perspective and so, its value is present in its lack of bias. Still, it limitations rise from the inability to provide an alternate point of view. Because of this, one is unable to determine whether it is completely factual. Finally, the article is valuable in regards to its content because it provides context about both the origins of penicillin *and* its direct effects on World War II, thus supplementing credibility. The content has its limitations because it doesn't provide detailed statistical data that may be necessary to answer the prompt at hand. Nonetheless, its explicit nature *does* provide insight into the extensivity of the effects.

The second source is a scholarly article which analyzes an extract from Alexander Fleming's laboratory journal describing his experimental results. This secondary source is a historical research narrative written by John S. Mailer, Jr., and Barbara Mason of Northern Illinois University. The lab entry provided in the narrative was published in Volume X, p. 226 of The British Journal of Experimental Pathology in May 1929. This origin is valuable because it contains a primary source within it, subsequently increasing its credibility. The date on which the narrative was written is unknown, but this limitation is aided by the lab entry's value and ability to provide a credible perspective. Though the authors' background is unknown (and therefore the article has the potential to be opinionated), it can be deemed relatively unbiased because it is written by collegiate individuals. Furthermore, in regards to the article's content, it holds value in its ability to quantitatively answer the question at hand. However, limitations are present in its lack of specificity, as it is not written with the context of the Allied forces in WWII.

Section II

World War II marked a turning point not only for war tactics and technological advancements, but also for the pharmaceutical industry. The new medical techniques developed between 1939 and 1945 targeted injuries related to the upbringing of new weaponry. Although penicillin was discovered in the years prior to the war, its industrialization in the early '40s was

98

extremely beneficial to the Allied forces' mortality rate due to: its ability to fight infections, its superiority over M&B sulfonamides, and its political effects on the Axis powers.

Initially, penicillin was deemed insignificant during the 1930s, as most people were focused on lifting themselves out of the Great Depression rather than adopting the use of this drug. However, once the number of Allied casualties began to rise exponentially, the American government was forced to embrace it on a wide-scale basis and implement its mass production. Soon, British and American scientists expanded penicillin's use out of laboratories and into the battlefields after discovering its ability to treat wounds. According to CNN, World War II resulted in between 50 and 80 million Allied deaths, of which about 25 million were due to war-related diseases (Smith). These diseases were mostly bacterial infections which were often fatal due to the unsanitary environment in which the troops were in. The extent to which penicillin benefited the Allies is elucidated through its effects on two prevalent infections: gangrene and septicemia. Gangrene is a disease in which tissue dies due to the lack of a sufficient blood supply. Because this had become an increasingly fatal disease for the soldiers, supplies of penicillin were sent with the troops making the D-day landings in June of 1944. According to a scholarly journal article published in the US National Library of Medicine, "the use of penicillin to treat gangrene prevented the need for roughly 20 to 30 thousand amputations" (Quinn). Additionally, penicillin was used to prevent septicemia or, blood poisoning. This infection could occur if patients underwent operations with equipment that hadn't been properly sterilized or if they were treated in a hospital where bacteria could be spread easily from person to person. By treating open wounds with penicillin, however, doctors were able to revitalize troops more quickly. This also reduced the treatment time, further preventing the spread of disease between units. In other words, penicillin was beneficial to the Allies because it could be used as a direct form of treatment, thus preventing the loss of limb and/ or the loss of life. Furthermore, another way in which penicillin's ability to fight infection was beneficial to the Allies lied in its ability to reduce the wait time between when a soldier was wounded and when they were seen by a doctor for surgery or treatment. According to history.com, before the industrialization of penicillin, this wait time was about 14 hours (Parker). The necessity for amputation is directly proportional to the amount of time an individual waits before seeking medical attention, as this only makes the body more susceptible to infection. Therefore, the administration of penicillin drastically reduced the probability that the wound would get infected and increased the survival rate of Allied soldiers.

Next, the industrialization of penicillin was extremely beneficial to the Allied forces due to its superiority over the previously-commercialized M&B sulfonamides (known today as Sulfapyridine). These drugs were introduced shortly after the discovery of penicillin in the 1930s. At first, they seemed to be the cure for all diseases and their production was in high demand for roughly 10 years. However, this was due to the fact that there were no testing requirements present at the time and the antibacterial's consequential effects were elucidated in 1937. Because of the lack of clinical research between this time and the onset of World War II, at least 100 people were poisoned with diethylene glycol, a fatal organic compound present in the medication. Although these risks were present, many army doctors continued to treat patients with the sulfa tablets up until the introduction of penicillin. After the elixir sulfanilamide disaster, the Federal Food, Drug, and Cosmetic Act was passed in 1938. Penicillin, unlike the M&B sulfonamides underwent a series of clinical trials before being approved for use on the battlefield. For example, results published in August 1941 in the medical journal "The Lancet" showed that four of five patients survived their various illnesses after being treated with penicillin. Conclusively, because penicillin superseded the sulfa drugs, its introduction to Allied troops can be deemed beneficial.

Finally, the mass production of penicillin had several political effects on the Axis powers which indirectly resulted in a decrease in the Allied mortality rate. Although penicillin had repeatedly proven to hold potential by 1942, countries like Germany did not seek to develop similar drugs. As previously mentioned, the Allies suffered from many bacterial diseases to which they fought with penicillin. According to the online German newspaper *Der Spiegel*, the Germans also suffered from similar diseases during World War II (Crossland). However, their lack of effort towards the battle against infection indirectly benefited the Allies. A journal article written in November of 1949 stated that "penicillin's immediate impact was to lessen wartime deaths, at least for the United States and its allies. During World War II, the Allies had penicillin in their arsenal of weapons, but Germany and its allies did not" (Hill). The Axis powers *had* begun to use variations of the M&B sulfonamides, but they were not nearly as beneficial as penicillin. As said by scholar-historian Gilbert Shama, Germany never created "a central body to coordinate research and eliminate duplication of effort" (Shama). From an economic perspective, while the Allied powers put tens of millions of dollars towards the industrialization of penicillin, Germany only allocated $10,000 towards their presumed research on antimicrobial compounds.

From a statistical standpoint, according to a surgeon with the 21st Army Group, "Allied troops suffered from gangrene at a rate of 1.5 cases per thousand and they died about half as often as in the early years of the war. Meanwhile, as penicillin remained scarce, German prisoners mostly received sulfa drugs instead and suffered gangrene at a rate of 20 to 30 per thousand" (Conniff). This decline in German forces benefited the Allies in later battles due to their ability to efficiently treat a broad range of infections with penicillin. In summation, while the Germans' lack of penicillin did not have a direct effect on the decrease in the Allies' mortality rate, it provided the Allies with a significant tactical advantage which saved thousands of lives later in the war.

In summation, the industrialization of penicillin was evidently a large factor in reducing the Allies' mortality rate. Its multifaceted use against deadly battlefield diseases resulted in an efficient recovery for the troops and reduced the number of disease-related deaths. Additionally, its more advanced chemical makeup proved to be more beneficial in treating disease than the previously marketed sulfonamides while its exclusivity put the Allied forces at an advantage against Germany. Therefore, although these were not all direct factors in the drastic increase in survival rate, both the pharmaceutical and political aspects of the "Wonder Drug" held great significance during the second World War.

Section III

This process exposed me to the various strategies historians use to explore questions and to some of the challenges they face. Often, in order to answer complex questions, one must rely heavily on analytical reasoning. Through the investigation, I gained a deeper understanding of the methodology required to write a comprehensive analysis and the limitations that accompany such a paper.

First, because of the specificity associated with my research question, I was not able to find many primary sources. This was a limitation in itself but, more importantly, it shaped the way I conducted the investigation. Historians prefer to use primary sources because such material elucidates past happenings, thus allowing them to draw more accurate inferences-- although this makes the process more complicated, it adds more significance to the topic at hand. The secondary sources I used were not preferable due to their lack of detail. Nevertheless, the ones I used to research the effects of penicillin on Allied soldiers during World War II sustained their value. For example, I did not come across many biased articles, as most of them were written by health professionals and adhered to a scientific nature. Additionally, I obtained extracts from newspapers written in the late twentieth century. Although these articles were not written during the time period my question addressed, it provided a different perspective from the ones offered by modern-day analyses. To a historian, it is important to have a multifaceted approach to any given question to avoid any type of bias, whatsoever. For example, if I had only utilized entries from Allied soldiers' journals which discussed their personal opinion on penicillin, I would not have represented the entirety of the topic. So, I used observational data in addition to anecdotal evidence to provide a balanced argument. Of course, as with any aspect of life, it is impossible to cover each and every perspective, as some are more subjective than others. Thus, historians are inevitably selective when portraying historical knowledge. I was aware of this, but attempted to elude the issue by referencing both Allied and Axis accounts of penicillin use during the war.

Conclusively, the investigation not only provided me with newfound knowledge regarding the medicinal aspects of the Second World War, but it also explicated the approaches historians take when conducting a study and the impediments they may face when doing so.

Works Cited

Bradley, Jeremy. "Penicillin in WWII." Penicillin, Synonym,

    classroom.synonym.com/did-invention-penicillin-affect-world-war-ii-8709.html.

Conniff, Richard. "Penicillin: Wonder Drug of World War II." HistoryNet, 3 July 2017,

    www.historynet.com/penicillin-wonder-drug-world-war-ii.htm.

Crossland, David. "Germany Still Locates 40,000 War Casualties a Year - SPIEGEL ONLINE -

    International." Database of Fallen Soldiers, Spiegel Online, 8 May 2012,

    www.spiegel.de/international/germany/germany-tracing-its-war-dead-from-world-war-ii-

    a-832063.html.

Hill, Charles. "'Penicillin Shown to Cure Syphilis.'" New York Times, 16 Dec. 1949.

Mailer, John S, and Barbara Mason. "Penicillin: Medicine's Wartime Wonder Drug and Its

    Production at Peoria, Illinois." Penicillin, Illinois Periodicals Online,

    www.lib.niu.edu/2001/iht810139.html.

"Martindale: The Complete Drug Reference." Penicillin Interactions, Medicine Complete,

    www.medicinescomplete.com/mc/martindale/current/login.htm?uri=https%3A%2F%2F

    www.medicinescomplete.com%2Fmc%2Fmartindale%2Fcurrent%2F1-a16-10-g.htm.

Parker, Justin. "Penicillin Discovered." History.com, A&E Television Networks,

    www.history.com/this-day-in-history/penicillin-discovered.

Quinn, Roswell. "Rethinking Antibiotic Research and Development: World War II and the

    Penicillin Collaborative." American Journal of Public Health, American Public Health

    Association, Mar. 2013, www.ncbi.nlm.nih.gov/pmc/articles/PMC3673487/.

Smith, Marc. "World War II Fast Facts." CNN, Cable News Network, 17 Aug. 2017,

    www.cnn.com/2013/07/09/world/world-war-ii-fast-facts/index.html.

5. EXAMPLE FIVE (23/25)

Name: 'To what extent did the philosophies of Dr. Martin Luther King, Jr. and Malcolm X align during the Civil Rights Movement between 1954 and 1968?

Author: Anonymous

Session: May 2022

Level: HL

Section 1: Identification and Evaluation of Sources

This investigation will explore the question: To what extent were the philosophies of Martin Luther King, Jr. and Malcolm X aligned during the Civil Rights Movement from 1954 to 1968? This is an important question because it challenges our ideas of civil rights figures as one-dimensional by showing the evolution of their ideas over time. The scope of this investigation focuses on the most prominent years of the Civil Rights Movement and the words and actions of Martin Luther King, Jr. and Malcolm X in that time, especially as their views changed near the ends of their lives.

Dr. Martin Luther King, Jr., *I Have A Dream*

Dr. Martin Luther King's renowned speech, *I Have A Dream*, is one primary source I examined. Its origins, being written by Dr. King himself in 1963, make it valuable to historians. Its purpose was to inspire change, while the content of the speech specifically addressed civil rights problems. These elements add value to historians by clearly defining the most significant issues of the time. However, due to time constraints and the level of publicity of the speech, the content was limited to be easily digestible to the American populus. Divisive issues wouldn't have held the focus of the speech, as it had an intention to unite people around the cause of civil rights.

In this investigation, *I Have A Dream* provides a basis of King's beliefs, which can be compared to his later beliefs. The speech contains what King considered the most valuable and impactful messages for the crowd and for the US Government to hear. These messages, which sum up the core of his philosophies, will be crucial in the investigation of the evolution of King's teachings and beliefs.

Malcolm X, *The Ballot or the Bullet*

One of the most famous orations given by Malcolm X, *The Ballot or the Bullet*, was presented at King Solomon Baptist Church, Detroit, Michigan, 12 April 1964. The timing of the speech is significant - it was given after his separation from the Nation of Islam (NOI), yet before his pilgrimage to Mecca. Malcolm X's views on black nationalism were noticeably changed after seeing the racial diversity in Mecca. Therefore, this speech provides an example to historians of his original, personal philosophy of black separatism and nationalism.

Malcolm X's intention in the speech was to clarify his own religious and political standing after breaking away from Nation of Islam, as well as call on African American listeners to join organizations promoting black nationalism as a means of obtaining black social and economic progression. He spoke to an African American audience, and his choices of content and rhetoric can be analyzed under that context.

The Ballot or the Bullet aims scathing criticism toward nonviolent integration efforts, but is limited in that it does not address the successes of these demonstrations. Malcolm utilizes historical examples of revolution and nationalism to support his message, but not examples of successful racial diversity. As he would see in Mecca, the aforementioned absence limits the audience's understanding of global capabilities to integrate and be universally accepting.

Section 2: Investigation and Analysis

Dr. Martin Luther King, Jr. and Malcolm X are commonly known as the embodiments of two opposing ideologies during the civil rights movement. However, this satisfying and simplistic image does not capture the full extent of their individual journeys, progressions, and changes that led, ultimately, toward one another.

their own people. It is evident that Malcolm X had a firm belief in achieving freedom, justice, and equality through principles of self-determination and black nationalism.

As their ideas and the civil rights movement progressed, King's messages moved beyond civil rights to address topics such as militancy, global imperialism, and poverty before his death. In speeches such as "Beyond Vietnam" given in 1967, or "The Other America" in 1968, King's ideas are more radical, signaling a convergence with and sometimes echoing the ideas that Malcolm X had previously expressed. For example, in "The Other America", King states "The fact is that freedom is never voluntarily given by the oppressor. It must be demanded by the oppressed - that's the long, sometimes tragic and turbulent story of history"(King, "The Other America"). We see a similar expression that a revolution, in this case a revolution more of values and legislation than bloodshed, but still markedly more intense than his earlier expressions, is being called for just as Malcolm X had called for in 1963.

After the assassination of Malcolm X in 1965, historian and theologian James H. Cone writes that King took a "... radical turn away from his vision of the American dream and to gaze at the horror of Malcolm's nightmare" (Cone), The statement alludes to his earlier explanation in the real difference between the two leaders: "King saw in America a dream as yet largely unfulfilled, Malcolm X saw a realized nightmare;" (Raines). King's disillusionment with his original vision and philosophy may have been impacted by Malcolm X's death; nevertheless, we see a definite change in his belief in the moral stability of the United States and its extension of Manifest Destiny. That is, "America was no longer good because God ordained America to be such, but America had major problems - flaws it must face to be the country it claimed to be" (Johnson, "The evolution of a King"). His speech "Beyond Vietnam" is evidence of these claims,

In the early 1950s and 60s we can see the original philosophies of each leader. Chosen to head the Montgomery Bus Boycott following Rosa Parks's arrest, King stated in December 1955: "We are here, we are here this evening because we're tired now. And I want to say that we are not here advocating violence. We have never done that. I want it to be known throughout Montgomery and throughout this nation that we are a Christian people ... The only weapon that we have in our hands this evening is the weapon of protest. That's all." (King, "Montgomery Bus Boycott"). Here, King relied on nonviolent protest and the principles of Christianity to promote the civil rights of African Americans. These themes would continue in his orations throughout the civil rights movement, with Christianity and nonviolent protest forming the cornerstone of his philosophy.

After his release from prison, Malcolm X moved to Chicago and became a minister in the NOI, as well as abandoned his surname in favor of "X", to symbolize the culture and identity stolen from African Americans by white oppression and slavery. In his sermons and speeches, Malcolm actively rejected King's notion of nonviolence, stating in his speech "A Message to the Grassroots" in November 1963 "There's no such thing as a nonviolent revolution. The only kind of revolution that's nonviolent is the Negro revolution. The only revolution based on loving your enemy is the Negro revolution. ... That's no revolution"(X, "A Message to the Grassroots"). In the same speech he uses other recent and historical revolutions to emphasize revolution, even bloody revolution, as the end solution to the problem of the black man in America. He also references the double standard of acceptable violence in drafting and sending African-Americans to war abroad when Afican-Americans in America stuck to a policy of nonviolence in defending

112

as he exposes the unsettling duplicity that the United States undertook by interfering in Vietnam in the name of civil and human rights. King also expands the issue of human rights to an international level by addressing these issues abroad, which would also be mirrored by Malcolm X.

Toward the end of his life, Malcolm X's philosophies took a turn as well - in his case due to a life-changing pilgrimage to Mecca. In April of 1964, Malcolm had broken away from the NOI and travelled to Mecca, where he witnessed "pilgrims of all colors from all parts of this earth displaying a spirit of unity and brotherhood like I've never seen before" (X, 1964 cited "Timeline of Malcolm X's Life"). His transformation is accentuated by the new name he received in his pilgrimage, El-Hajj Malik El-Shabazz. After experiencing a place of racial equality, mutual respect, and dignity, Malcolm departed from his previous ideal of black nationalism, separatism, and supremacy in favor of a broader movement against white supremacy. His journey granted him greater optimism concerning a solution to the racial inequality of the United States. After returning, he stated that "America is the first country ... that can actually have a bloodless revolution" (X, 1964 cited "Malcolm X Biography"), which stands out in stark contrast to his earlier insistence in "A Message to the Grassroots" of the exact opposite.

The widespread perspective of Martin Luther King, Jr. as the man with "a dream" and moderate advocate for nonviolence is true to an extent, but is not a fair and comprehensive picture of his life and philosophies. The view of Malcolm X as a radical black separatist and supremacist is again true, and yet again fails to acknowledge the evolution of his ideas thinking this. This perspective is only true of small moments in time, and does not allow a more complex exploration of the humanity and changes of the two leaders. Martin Luther King, Jr. did preach nonviolence and a hope for a better world where all people would be judged not "... by the color of their skin, but by the content of their character" (King, "I Have A Dream"), a lasting image dedicated to a world full of opportunity and equality. As he pursued this dream, the deeply rooted flaws in American society that stood in its way became more apparent, leading him to a more direct and alienating approach, identifying problems on a global scale and losing trust in the moral character of white Americans.

Malcolm X's philosophy was, at its core, always one of dignifying the black man, bringing self-respect and unity to the African American people, and advancing their social, political, and economic position. Though his ideas can be divided into before and after Mecca, his end goal stayed the same. Just as Martin Luther King, Jr.'s approach to achieving his dream changed, Malcolm X's changed as well. His preaching of anti-white and black supremacist ideals were not the main purpose of his message, and even further, were components of the NOI that he later departed from.

Malcolm X and Martin Luther King, Jr. were united in their desire for the freedom of African-Americans. They were equally unhappy with the current state of race in the United States and wanted to uplift those they saw struggling under oppression. Their approaches began diametrically different, but over the course of time gravitated toward one another as they acknowledged the shortcomings in their initial approach and changed accordingly.

The philosophies of Malcolm X and Dr. Martin Luther King, Jr. align to a certain extent over the period of 1954 to 1968. Their beliefs were always focused on the freedom of the oppressed, specifically African-Americans. They both called for a revolution of the American mindset - a political, social, and economic revolution. Although the progression of their philosophies did not line up with each other in their time period, their words carry on their shared legacy of uplifting the African-American people.

Section 3: Reflection

In this investigation I used both primary and secondary sources to examine the perspectives and philosophies of Martin Luther King, Jr. and Malcolm X. Primary sources were often limited by their timing, occurring before or after important events and thereafter being altered in significance and meaning. Secondary sources, which possessed the benefit of a full picture of what would and did happen, could be limited in their interpretation of events, only examined what supported their view.

The ability to assess the reliability of sources is paramount to the career of a historian. Reliable sources can be evaluated based on the education and experience of the author, date, content, and other factors. When choosing secondary sources, I researched the qualifications of the authors to assess the reliability of the source. With primary sources, I frequently was challenged by examining the context of the speeches I read, including what had happened or been said before, who was being spoken to, and how the speech is viewed by current historians. Historians need to have more than a surface level knowledge of events that occurred to produce a meaningful interpretation of them. In my investigation, I learned about the depth of research required to fully understand a point in history.

Furthermore, understanding prominent leaders and figures in history is even more difficult. People are incredibly complex - they grow, learn, change, come from different backgrounds, have different motives, and emotions. In my research I was specifically interested in these factors and the changes they created. A method I used to approach this was comparing texts written by the same person at different times. Historians can assess these changes by being aware of when ideas were first publicly introduced, indicating the beginning of their development. I used this to examine Malcolm X and Martin Luther King, Jr.'s speeches, particularly noting the progression of themes throughout. One can never truly know how a person felt or why they acted a certain way, but through an examination of available sources a historian must attempt to understand the factors that have shaped people and history through imagination and empathy.

Works Cited

Cone, James H. "Malcolm X: The Impact of a Cultural Revolutionary." *The Christian Century*,

    Vol. 109, No. 38, December 23,30, 1992, pp. 1189-1195.

Daniels, Antonio Maurice, Dr. "Malcolm X's 'The Ballot or the Bullet': A

    Summary."*Revolutionary Paideia*.

    revolutionarypaideia.com/2013/02/09/malcolm-xs-the-ballot-or-the-bullet-a-thorough-su

    mmary/

Desmond-Harris, Jenée. "The Poor People's Campaign: the little-known protest MLK was

    planning when he died." *Vox.* 18 January 2015.

    www.vox.com/2015/1/18/7548453/poor-peoples-campaign-mlk

Johnson, Andre E. "The evolution of a King." *MLK50.com* 22 March 2018.

    mlk50.com/the-evolution-of-a-king-3185c754fca1

Johnson, Andre E. and Stone, Anthony J., Jr. "'The Most Dangerous Negro in America':

    Rhetoric, Race, and the Prophetic Pessimism of Martin Luther King Jr." *Journal of*

    Communication and Religion, Vol. 21, 2017, pp. 987-988.

King, Martin L., Jr. "Beyond Vietnam." 4 April 1967, New York, New York. Audio Speech. *The*

    Martin Luther King, Jr. Research and Education Institute.

    kinginstitute.stanford.edu/king-papers/documents/beyond-vietnam

King, Martin L., Jr. "I Have A Dream." Lincoln Memorial, Washington, D.C. 28 August 1963.

    American Rhetoric. www.americanrhetoric.com/speeches/mlkihaveadream.htm

King, Martin L., Jr. "The Montgomery Bus Boycott." 5 December 1955, Holt Street Baptist

    Church, Montgomery, AL. *Black Past.*

www.blackpast.org/african-american-history/speeches-african-american-history/1955-ma

rtin-luther-king-jr-montgomery-bus-boycott/

King, Martin L., Jr. "Nonviolence: The Only Road to Freedom." 4 May 1966. *Teaching*

American History.

teachingamericanhistory.org/library/document/nonviolence-the-only-road-to-freedom/

King, Martin L., Jr. "The Other America." 14 March 1968, Grosse Pointe High School, Grosse

Pointe, MI. *Beacon Broadside*. 10 March 2018.

www.beaconbroadside.com/broadside/2018/03/martin-luther-king-jrs-the-other-america-s

till-radical-50-years-later.html

"Malcolm X." *The Martin Luther King, Jr. Research and Education Institute*.

kinginstitute.stanford.edu/encyclopedia/malcolm-x

"Malcolm X Biography." *The Biography.com*. 2 April 2014. A&E Television Networks.

www.biography.com/activist/malcolm-x

Raines, Robert A. "Closer Than We Knew." *The New York Times*. 17 March 1991.

www.nytimes.com/1991/03/17/books/closer-than-we-knew.html

"Timeline of Malcolm X's Life." *American Experience*.

www.pbs.org/wgbh/americanexperience/features/malcolmx-timeline-malcolm-xs-life/

X, Malcolm. "The Ballot or the Bullet." 12 April 1964, King Solomon Baptist Church, Detroit,

MI. *American RadioWorks*.

americanradioworks.publicradio.org/features/blackspeech/mx.html

X, Malcolm. "A Message to the Grassroots." 10 November 1963, Northern Negro Grass Roots

Leadership Conference, King Solomon Baptist Church, Detroit, MI. *Malcolm X.*

malcolmxfiles.blogspot.com/2013/06/a-message-to-grassroots-november-10-1963.html

X, Malcolm, and Alex Haley. 1965. The autobiography of Malcolm X. New York: Grove Press.

6. EXAMPLE SIX (25/25)

Name: "To what extent was the victory of the Christian Democratic Party in the Italian general election, on 18th April 1948, due to US intervention in the campaign?"

Author: Anonymous

Session: May 2021

Level: HL

Contents

Criteria A: Identification and evaluation of sources

The focus of this investigation is the research question: "To what extent was the victory of the Christian Democratic Party in the Italian general election, on 18th April 1948, due to US intervention in the campaign?" A primary source relevant to the investigation is a telegram sent by the US Ambassador in Italy James Dunn to the US Secretary General G. Marshall on 16th March 1948. The source is relevant because it offers insight into an official diplomatic position at the time of the election campaign and is from an authoritative figure in Italy. A relevant secondary source is historian William Blum's book 'Killing Hope: U.S. Military and CIA Interventions since World War II'. The book offers this investigation an analysis of US intervention in Italy, and puts its involvement in 1948 into a broader context and benefits from hindsight.

A value of the origin of the telegram is that it offers insight into what the US was told about the situation in Italy and outlines the potential response to a left-wing victory in the Italian election of 1948. A value of its purpose is that, as a confidential communication, Dunn can be direct and frank in his recommendations. A value of the content is that Dunn's diplomatic position means that he was informed about events occurring in Italy and outlines factors that may have shaped US intervention in the election.

A limitation of the origin is that as a US diplomat Dunn may not fully appreciate the social and cultural sentiments involved in Italian politics and may be influenced by the Truman administration's position on containing Communism in Europe, thus exaggerating the threat it posed in Italy. A limitation of its purpose is that the telegram merely briefs and advises and it also does not reveal the extent to which Dunn's views influenced the US government's policy. A limitation of the content is that it focuses on the potential 'threat' by left-wing parties and lacks balance in terms of popular sentiment and the role of center and right-wing parties.

A value of the origin of the publication by William Blum is that it was written by an expert on US foreign policy, whose publications have been recognised as authoritative on the subject by historians such as Noam Chomsky.[1] The publication date, 2003,[2] implies that Blum had the benefit of hindsight and that he could access government sources that were restricted up to the 1990s. A value of the purpose is that as an academic study, Blum may attempt to offer a balanced analysis of events. A value of the content is that Blum had access to declassified CIA reports and government documents and gives examples of when and how the US intervened.[3]

A limitation of the origin is that Blum is critical of US interventions and this may lead to a lack of objectivity in his account.[4] A limitation of the purpose is that the book covers a broad scope of US intervention sand intends to find parallels between involvement in the Italian election and other intervention. A limitation of the content is that Blum's analysis is primarily focused on US interests and actions, and therefore the role of Italian domestic aspects in determining the outcome of the election are marginalised.

---

[1] "Killing Hope U.S. Military and CIA Interventions since World War II," William Blum, accessed May 13, 2017, https://williamblum.org/books/killing-hope

[2] William Blum, *Killing Hope: US Military and CIA Interventions since World War II* (Zed Books, 2003), accessed October 25, 2017, https://books.google.co.uk/books?hl=it&lr=&id=-IbQvd13uToC&oi=fnd&pg=PA3&ots=cJqbNeFmhH&sig=zTMCJKWDtdUvoXgwQiF_RYdSMNw&redir_esc=y#v=onepage&q&f=false

[3] William Blum, "Italy, 1947-1948: Free Elections, Hollywood-style," in *Killing Hope: U.S. Military and CIA Interventions since World War II*, accessed October 24, 2017, https://williamblum.org/chapters/killing-hope/italy

[4] "Killing Hope U.S. Military and CIA Interventions since World War II," William Blum, accessed May 13, 2017, https://williamblum.org/books/killing-hope

Criteria B: Investigation

The events leading to the victory of the Christian Democratic Party in the Italian general election of 18th April 1948 [5] were deeply controversial and went on to shape the country in the post-war period. The election was focused on two possible political outcomes, a victory by the Popular Democratic Front (FP), a left-wing coalition which united the Communist Party (PCI), the Socialist Party (PSI) and other left-wing groups, or a victory by the Christian Democrats (DC), a liberal party led by Alcide De Gasperi. [6] The outcome of the election, 48% in favour of the DC and 31% in favour of the FP, [7] was significant as it shifted political control away from the left in a nation that many believed was inclined to become a socialist state.[8] The controversy of the election lies in the role of the US, who promoted the DC through covert operations, financial assistance and propaganda. [9] Although historian Noam Chomsky suggests that US action was pivotal in determining the result of the election, historians such as James Miller claim that the defeat of the FP was primarily due to the coalition's weaknesses, and to the DC's inherent strengths.

It could be argued that US intervention was significant in determining the outcome of the election, as it made the defeat of the left inevitable. Historian Noam Chomsky, argues that the key method used by the US to manipulate the result was economic pressure. [10] In 1947 Italy became a recipient

---

[5] James Edward Miller, *The United States and Italy, 1940-1950: The Politics and Diplomacy of Stabilization*, 248, https://www.questiaschool.com/read/98449704/the-united-states-and-italy-1940-1950-the-politics
[6] Francesco Bonini, *La Grande Contrapposizione: Aspetti delle Elezioni del 1948 a Reggio Emilia* (n.p.: Tecnograph, 1990)

[7] Blum, *Killing Hope*, 34

[8] Central Intelligence Agency, 54. *Weekly Summary Excerpt, 30 December 1947, Prospects for Communist Action in Italy*, December 30, 1947, accessed February 17, 2017, https://www.cia.gov/library/center-for-the-study-of-intelligence/csi-publications/books-and-monographs/assessing-the-soviet-threat-the-early-cold-war-years/5563bod2.pdf

[9] James Edward Miller, "Taking off the Gloves: The United States and the Italian Elections of 1948," *Diplomatic History* 7, no. 1 (January 1983): accessed March 14, 2017, doi:10.1111/j.1467-7709.1983.tb00381.x

[10] Noam Chomsky, "Noam Chomsky on the Long History of US Meddling in Foreign Elections," interview by C. J. Polychroniou, *Truthout*, January 19, 2017, accessed March 12, 2017, https://chomsky.info/20170119/

of the European Recovery Program and by 1948 it depended on US material aid. [11] However, in 1947 the US government threatened to terminate this aid if there was a 'Communist victory' in 1948. [12] In his Marshall Plan speech in June 1947, G. Marshall, declared that if "political parties… which… perpetuate human misery" took power in recipient countries, ERP aid to those nations would be terminated. [13] This economic coercion was articulated after the Truman administration declared that $227 million was appropriated for interim aid, and would be sent to Italy to help redress its post-war recession but only following a 'Communist' defeat in the election. [14] This put pressure on the FP, leading to internal divisions, [15] and influenced the opinion of Italian voters, who realised that a left-wing victory would be economically devastating. [16] Additionally, as the Soviets did not want parties affiliated to them to receive Marshall aid, this exacerbated the splits within the FP. [17] Umberto Terracini, co-leader of the PCI, argued that the ERP was fundamental for Italy's development.[18]

---

[11] Miller, *The United*, 213,

[12] James Clement Dunn to George C. Marshall, telegram, March 16, 1948, accessed March 14, 2017, https://history.state.gov/historicaldocuments/frus1948v03/d526

[13] George Catlett Marshall, "The Marshall Plan Speech," speech, June 1947, marshallfoundation.org, accessed February 21, 2017, http://marshallfoundation.org/marshall/the-marshall-plan/marshall-plan-speech/

[14] Stefano Luconi, "Anticommunism, Americanization, and Ethnic Identity: Italian Americans and the 1948 Parliamentary Elections in Italy," *The Historian* 62, no. 2 (2000): https://www.questiaschool.com/read/1G1-60578630/anticommunism-americanization-and-ethnic-identity

[15] Alessandro Brogi, *Confronting America: The Cold War between the United States and the Communists in France and Italy* (Chapel Hill, NC: University of North Carolina Press, 2011), 91, https://www.questiaschool.com/read/121593351/confronting-america-the-cold-war-between-the-united

[16] Ibid, 97

[17] Ibid, 91

[18] Ibid, 92

Indeed, the US government also supported the DC through covert CIA operations and other economic inducements. [19] Millions of dollars were channeled to the DC between 1947 and 1948; for instance, on 8th January 1947, the US government released $50 million to De Gasperi. [20] The US used its economic power to threaten supporters of the FP and to show that a left-wing victory would be economic suicide. The US also ensured that the DC had adequate resources to pursue a comprehensive propaganda campaign of its own. [21] Furthermore, the US government encouraged American Labor Unions, comprising of members of Italian descent, to send funds to anti-Communist parties in Italy. One influential union was the Ladies Garment Workers Union, which numbered 40,000 Italian members [22] and provided the Social Democratic Party, which split from its radical faction in 1947, with $200,000 for its election campaign. [23] These funds allowed Italian parties to make investments in anti-left propaganda, which was key to manipulating public opinion. The economic aid provided to Italy allowed the US to position itself as the only power that could lead the nation out of crisis [24] and this enabled it to manipulate voters' opinions. [25] The US government was open about its alignment with the DC and with De Gasperi. On 31st May 1947, after De Gasperi

---

[19] "Case Study: Italian Elections and CIA Founding," in *Understanding the hidden side of government*, ed. Loch K. Johnson, vol. 1, *Strategic Intelligence* (Praeger Security International, 2006), 37-38, accessed February 28, 2017, https://books.google.co.uk/books?id=cg39hcj6AxQC&pg=RA2-PA37&lpg=RA2-PA37&dq=cia+payments+to+italian+democratic+party+1948&source=bl&ots=QHIkmVNvo_&sig=0pnF54Brr6bAKdf6pgkNKJNxa18&hl=en&sa=X&ved=0ahUKEwifvZb8oLPSAhWqAMAKHVlVAE8Q6AEIODAF#v=onepage&q

[20] Miller, *The United*, 248

[21] "Case Study" 37-38

[22] Luconi, "Anticommunism, Americanization"

[23] Ibid

[24] Blum, *Killing Hope*, 30-31

[25] Miller, "Taking off the Gloves"

returned from a business trip to the US, he excluded left-wing parties from his coalition. [26] This was explained as a recommendation from the Truman administration which in return offered increased financial aid and cancelled the Italian debt to the US of $1 billion. [27]

Additionally, the US government was able to use the Roman Catholic Church as a tool of anti-left propaganda. [28] As Italy was predominantly Catholic, the Pope played a significant role in how political parties were portrayed. In January 1948, Pius XII asked the archbishop of New York for advice on how to approach the Italian political situation; the archbishop responded that the Pope should continue delivering anti-left speeches. [29] This was advice that Pius XII followed. [30] In one speech he made referencing the election the Pope declared "In this year of... threats... the time for Christian conscience has come". [31]

Furthermore, the US used the threat of military action to influence the outcome of the election. In February 1948, [32] the Truman administration laid contingency plans for military involvement in case of a left-wing victory. [33] This consisted of sending military aid to support underground operations in Italy to counter Communist forces. [34] Additionally, during the campaign, US warships were often

---

[26] Blum, *Killing Hope*, 29

[27] Miller, *The United*, 214

[28] Blum, *Killing Hope*, 30

[29] Brogi, *Confronting America*, 103
[30] Ibid

[31] Pius XII Pope, "Discorso Di Sua Santità Al Popolo Romano," speech, March 28, 1948, w2.vatican, accessed May 14, 2017, http://w2.vatican.va/content/pius-xii/it/speeches/1948/documents/hf_p-xii_spe_19480328_popolo-romano.html

[32] "Secret 1948 Role Disclosed by the U.S.," *The New York Times*, February 11, 1948, accessed May 14, 2017, https://www.cia.gov/library/readingroom/docs/CIA-RDP85B00236R000100150005-3.pdf

[33] Miller, "Taking off the Gloves"

[34] Noam Chomsky, "Restoring the Traditional Order," in *What Uncle Sam Really Wants* (n.p.: Odonian Press, 1992)

found anchored in Italian ports. [35] Indeed, military intimidations persuaded many Italians to vote for

the DC as there was no public appetite for another conflict that would throw Italy into crisis. [36]

However, it could be argued that US intervention in the Italian election did not determine its

outcome and that the key factor was the weakness of the FP. The exclusion of left-wing parties from

De Gasperi's cabinet [37] undermined their political credibility. Additionally, the FP failed to gain

assurance of economic support from the USSR that could counter US threats to remove aid. [38]

Indeed the FP's campaign also attacked the Marshall Plan and the Church, which proved deeply

unpopular, [39] as by 1948 most Italians were pro-American and pro-Roman Catholic. Pietro Secchia,

co-leader of the PCI, [40] stated that the US was the "organizer of sabotage and betrayal." [41] Historian

Alessandro Brogi argues that the FP's anti-Marshall campaign was disastrous as it threatened

"economic promise" and recovery. [42]

---

[35] Blum, *Killing Hope*, 31

[36] National Security Council, NSC 5/2, (Wash. 1948). Accessed May 14, 2017.
https://history.state.gov/historicaldocuments/frus1948v04/d28

[37] Blum, *Killing Hope*, 29

[38] Brogi, *Confronting America*, 92-97

[39] Miller, "Taking off the Gloves"

[40] Robert Ventresca, *From Fascism to Democracy: Culture and Politics in the Italian Election of 1948* (2004), 174, accessed March 11, 2017,
https://books.google.co.uk/books?id=OKA6i7SenW0C&pg=PA168&lpg=PA168&dq=weaknesses+of+the+PCI+in+1948&source=bl&ots=BNYTV0L9aa&sig=FHiuigJieiNTkT8wrellfuT9YZY&hl=it&sa=X&ved=0ahUKEwiD7uuI487SAhWIJ8AKHc1bBpYQ6AEIMDAC#v=onepage&q=

[41] Brogi, *Confronting America*, 104

[42] Ibid, 87

In addition, although divisions within the FP were exacerbated by US intervention, it was already deeply divided and its popularity was diminishing. When the coalition was established, a faction of the PSI split from the Socialist Party [43] and this undermined its stability. Historian James Miller argues that the FP was in a state of complete chaos by 1940. [44] The FP was unable to secure adequate funding to compete with the DC in terms of propaganda. Then, on March 20th 1948, after a declaration on the status of Trieste by Britain, France and the US, which called for the return of the area to Italian administration, Stalin opposed it and took Yugoslavia's side. [45] This was a death blow politically for the PCI as it became the party associated with a power that opposed historic Italian territorial interests. [46]

Finally, historian Robert Ventresca claims that the inherent strengths of the DC may have been the deciding factor in its victory. [47] The party invested effectively in its propaganda and relentlessly depicted the FP as 'godless'. [48] De Gasperi's ability as a leader was also exploited. Ventresca argues that De Gasperi was "indispensable to his... party" as he capably managed disparate groups within it. [49] In addition, it was De Gasperi who invited the Church's attacks on Communism and manipulated

---

[43] Miller, *The United*, 220

[44] Ibid

[45] Miller, "Taking off the Gloves"

[46] Ibid

[47] Robert Ventresca, *In God's Country: State, Society and Democracy in the Italian Election of 1948* (National Library of Canada, 2000), accessed March 14, 2017, http://www.collectionscanada.gc.ca/obj/s4/f2/dsk2/ftp03/NQ49908.pdf

[48] Ventresca, *From Fascism*, 200

[49] Ventresca, *In God's*, 70

the pulpit to depict the choice of April 1948 as one between 'Christianity and atheism'. [50] This led

voters to believe they needed to put their faith first at the ballot box. [51]

In conclusion, the weaknesses of the FP, De Gasperi's leadership and the support of the Catholic

Church for the DC were crucial factors in determining the outcome of the Italian general election of

1948. It is however reasonable to conclude that the extensive intervention of the US government,

through economic incentives and assistance, was a major factor in persuading Italians to vote for the

Christian Democrats. On 18th April 1948, Italians voted primarily to retain US economic support. The

threat of the cessation of ERP aid and of economic crisis, ultimately led to the FP's defeat.

Criteria C: Reflection

This investigation allowed me to better understand the methods used by historians.

I learned that there are obstacles when gathering a range of sources, and that accessing sensitive

primary material can be difficult. Although the Cold War has been written about extensively by

historians, the specific focus of my investigation was less well explored. As historians do, I had to

infer and cross reference material from experts, and CIA and military reports. It was also interesting

to see how historians reassess their perspectives when sources become available. Historian

Alessandro Brogi published his work in 2011 [52] and could access sources restricted up to the 1990s

which allowed him to write a more balanced account of events.

---

[50] Miller, *The United*, 248

[51] Ventresca, *In God's*, 3

[52] Blum, *Killing Hope*, 4

Selectivity is another challenge for historians and one I encountered in my investigation. As I developed my thematic arguments, I had to omit evidence such as details about exchanges of information between the US government and De Gasperi. I also had to be selective with secondary sources, and focused on the work of peer assessed, respected historians such as Noam Chomsky. Another obstacle highlighted to me was the potential cultural differences of historians themselves that needs to be appreciated. I worked with both English and Italian sources which revealed nuances in interpretations, particularly regarding religious-cultural factors. There are also challenges in the specialization of a historian; it was in fact difficult for me to interpret the economic data from the time as this is an area I do not study.

The need to evaluate sources was also highlighted to me as a key part of the historian's methodology, for example when using the CIA report titled 'Prospects for Communist Action in Italy' [53] as its content had to be assessed in line with the document's intent within the early Cold War context. Historian William Blum argues that US intervention led the DC to triumph, [54] while historian James Miller argues that the FP lost the election primarily due to its inherent weaknesses. [55] Both historians used similar evidence, but support different claims and this revealed how the use of reason and emotion is important in historians' methodology and how sources are interpreted; Historian Alessandro Brogi was born in Florence and was educated in Italy [56] and may have been influenced by national sentiments at the time when developing his account.

---

[53] Central Intelligence Agency, 54. *Weekly*

[54] Blum, *Killing Hope*, 27-34

[55] Miller, *The United*

[56] "Faculty Bio - Alessandro Brogi." uark.edu. Accessed March 9, 2017.
http://uark.edu/depts/histinfo/history/index.php/faculty_bio/2

Works cited list

Blum, William. "Italy, 1947-1948: Free Elections, Hollywood-style." In *Killing Hope: U.S. Military and CIA Interventions since World War II.* Accessed October 24, 2017. https://williamblum.org/chapters/killing-hope/italy.

Blum, William. *Killing Hope: US Military and CIA Interventions since World War II.* Zed Books, 2003. Accessed October 25, 2017. https://books.google.co.uk/books?hl=it&lr=&id=-IbQvd13uToC&oi=fnd&pg=PA3&ots=cJqbNeFmhH&sig=zTMCJKWDtdUvoXgwQiF_RYdSMNw &redir_esc=y#v=onepage&q&f=false.

Bonini, Francesco. *La Grande Contrapposizione: Aspetti delle Elezioni del 1948 a Reggio Emilia.* N.p.: Tecnograph, 1990.

Brogi, Alessandro. *Confronting America: The Cold War between the United States and the Communists in France and Italy.* Chapel Hill, NC: University of North Carolina Press, 2011. https://www.questiaschool.com/read/121593351/confronting-america-the-cold-war-between-the-united.

"Case Study: Italian Elections and CIA Founding." In *Understanding the hidden side of government,* edited by Loch K. Johnson, 37-38. Vol. 1 of *Strategic Intelligence.* Praeger Security International, 2006. Accessed February 28, 2017. https://books.google.co.uk/books?id=cg39hcj6AxQC&pg=RA2-PA37&lpg=RA2-PA37&dq=cia+payments+to+italian+democratic+party+1948&source=bl&ots=QHIkmVNvo_&sig=0pnF54Brr6bAKdf6pgkNKJNxa18&hl=en&sa=X&ved=0ahUKEwifvZb8oLPSAhWqAMAKH VIVAE8Q6AEIODAF#v=onepage&q.

Central Intelligence Agency. *54. Weekly Summary Excerpt, 30 December 1947, Prospects for Communist Action in Italy.* December 30, 1947. Accessed February 17, 2017. https://www.cia.gov/library/center-for-the-study-of-intelligence/csi-publications/books-and-monographs/assessing-the-soviet-threat-the-early-cold-war-years/5563bod2.pdf.

134

Chomsky, Noam. "Noam Chomsky on the Long History of US Meddling in Foreign Elections." Interview by C. J. Polychroniou. *Truthout,* January 19, 2017. Accessed March 12, 2017. https://chomsky.info/20170119/.

Chomsky, Noam. "Restoring the Traditional Order." In *What Uncle Sam Really Wants.* N.p.: Odonian Press, 1992.

Dunn, James Clement. Telegram to George C. Marshall, telegram, March 16, 1948. Accessed March 14, 2017. https://history.state.gov/historicaldocuments/frus1948v03/d526.

"Faculty Bio - Alessandro Brogi." uark.edu. Accessed March 9, 2017. http://uark.edu/depts/histinfo/history/index.php/faculty_bio/2.

"Killing Hope U.S. Military and CIA Interventions since World War II." William Blum. Accessed May 13, 2017. https://williamblum.org/books/killing-hope.

Luconi, Stefano. "Anticommunism, Americanization, and Ethnic Identity: Italian Americans and the 1948 Parliamentary Elections in Italy." *The Historian* 62, no. 2 (2000). https://www.questiaschool.com/read/1G1-60578630/anticommunism-americanization-and-ethnic-identity.

Marshall, George Catlett. "The Marshall Plan Speech." Speech, June 1947. marshallfoundation.org. Accessed February 21, 2017. http://marshallfoundation.org/marshall/the-marshall-plan/marshall-plan-speech/.

Miller, James Edward. "Taking off the Gloves: The United States and the Italian Elections of 1948." *Diplomatic History* 7, no. 1 (January 1983). Accessed March 14, 2017. https://doi.org/10.1111/j.1467-7709.1983.tb00381.x.

Miller, James Edward. *The United States and Italy, 1940-1950: The Politics and Diplomacy of Stabilization.* https://www.questiaschool.com/read/98449704/the-united-states-and-italy-1940-1950-the-politics.

7. EXAMPLE SEVEN (23/25)

Name: '"To what extent was the victory of the Christian Democratic Party in the Italian general election, on 18th April 1948, due to US intervention in the campaign?"

Author: Anonymous

Session: May 2022

Level: HL

Contents

Criteria A: Identification and evaluation of sources

The focus of this investigation is the research question: "To what extent was the victory of the Christian Democratic Party in the Italian general election, on 18th April 1948, due to US intervention in the campaign?" A primary source relevant to the investigation is a telegram sent by the US Ambassador in Italy James Dunn to the US Secretary General G. Marshall on 16th March 1948. The source is relevant because it offers insight into an official diplomatic position at the time of the election campaign and is from an authoritative figure in Italy. A relevant secondary source is historian William Blum's book 'Killing Hope: U.S. Military and CIA Interventions since World War II'. The book offers this investigation an analysis of US intervention in Italy, and puts its involvement in 1948 into a broader context and benefits from hindsight.

A value of the origin of the telegram is that it offers insight into what the US was told about the situation in Italy and outlines the potential response to a left-wing victory in the Italian election of 1948. A value of its purpose is that, as a confidential communication, Dunn can be direct and frank in his recommendations. A value of the content is that Dunn's diplomatic position means that he was informed about events occurring in Italy and outlines factors that may have shaped US intervention in the election.

A limitation of the origin is that as a US diplomat Dunn may not fully appreciate the social and cultural sentiments involved in Italian politics and may be influenced by the Truman administration's position on containing Communism in Europe, thus exaggerating the threat it posed in Italy. A limitation of its purpose is that the telegram merely briefs and advises and it also does not reveal the extent to which Dunn's views influenced the US government's policy. A limitation of the content is that it focuses on the potential 'threat' by left-wing parties and lacks balance in terms of popular

sentiment and the role of center and right-wing parties.

A value of the origin of the publication by William Blum is that it was written by an expert on US

foreign policy, whose publications have been recognised as authoritative on the subject by historians

such as Noam Chomsky. [1] The publication date, 2003, [2] implies that Blum had the benefit of

hindsight and that he could access government sources that were restricted up to the 1990s. A value

of the purpose is that as an academic study, Blum may attempt to offer a balanced analysis of

events. A value of the content is that Blum had access to declassified CIA reports and government

documents and gives examples of when and how the US intervened. [3]

A limitation of the origin is that Blum is critical of US interventions and this may lead to a lack of

objectivity in his account. [4] A limitation of the purpose is that the book covers a broad scope of US

intervention sand intends to find parallels between involvement in the Italian election and other

intervention. A limitation of the content is that Blum's analysis is primarily focused on US interests

and actions, and therefore the role of Italian domestic aspects in determining the outcome of the

election are marginalised.

---

[1] "Killing Hope U.S. Military and CIA Interventions since World War II," William Blum, accessed May 13, 2017, https://williamblum.org/books/killing-hope

[2] William Blum, *Killing Hope: US Military and CIA Interventions since World War II* (Zed Books, 2003), accessed October 25, 2017, https://books.google.co.uk/books?hl=it&lr=&id=-IbQvd13uToC&oi=fnd&pg=PA3&ots=cJqbNeFmhH&sig=zTMCJKWDtdUvoXgwQiF_RYdSMNw&redir_esc=y#v=onepage&q&f=false

[3] William Blum, "Italy, 1947-1948: Free Elections, Hollywood-style," in *Killing Hope: U.S. Military and CIA Interventions since World War II*, accessed October 24, 2017, https://williamblum.org/chapters/killing-hope/italy

[4] "Killing Hope U.S. Military and CIA Interventions since World War II," William Blum, accessed May 13, 2017, https://williamblum.org/books/killing-hope

Criteria B: Investigation

The events leading to the victory of the Christian Democratic Party in the Italian general election of 18th April 1948 [5] were deeply controversial and went on to shape the country in the post-war period. The election was focused on two possible political outcomes, a victory by the Popular Democratic Front (FP), a left-wing coalition which united the Communist Party (PCI), the Socialist Party (PSI) and other left-wing groups, or a victory by the Christian Democrats (DC), a liberal party led by Alcide De Gasperi. [6] The outcome of the election, 48% in favour of the DC and 31% in favour of the FP, [7] was significant as it shifted political control away from the left in a nation that many believed was inclined to become a socialist state.[8] The controversy of the election lies in the role of the US, who promoted the DC through covert operations, financial assistance and propaganda. [9] Although historian Noam Chomsky suggests that US action was pivotal in determining the result of the election, historians such as James Miller claim that the defeat of the FP was primarily due to the coalition's weaknesses, and to the DC's inherent strengths.

It could be argued that US intervention was significant in determining the outcome of the election, as it made the defeat of the left inevitable. Historian Noam Chomsky, argues that the key method used by the US to manipulate the result was economic pressure. [10] In 1947 Italy became a recipient

---

[5] James Edward Miller, *The United States and Italy, 1940-1950: The Politics and Diplomacy of Stabilization*, 248, https://www.questiaschool.com/read/98449704/the-united-states-and-italy-1940-1950-the-politics

[6] Francesco Bonini, *La Grande Contrapposizione: Aspetti delle Elezioni del 1948 a Reggio Emilia* (n.p.: Tecnograph, 1990)

[7] Blum, *Killing Hope*, 34

[8] Central Intelligence Agency, *54. Weekly Summary Excerpt, 30 December 1947, Prospects for Communist Action in Italy*, December 30, 1947, accessed February 17, 2017, https://www.cia.gov/library/center-for-the-study-of-intelligence/csi-publications/books-and-monographs/assessing-the-soviet-threat-the-early-cold-war-years/5563bod2.pdf

[9] James Edward Miller, "Taking off the Gloves: The United States and the Italian Elections of 1948," *Diplomatic History* 7, no. 1 (January 1983): accessed March 14, 2017, doi:10.1111/j.1467-7709.1983.tb00381.x

[10] Noam Chomsky, "Noam Chomsky on the Long History of US Meddling in Foreign Elections," interview by C. J. Polychroniou, *Truthout*, January 19, 2017, accessed March 12, 2017, https://chomsky.info/20170119/

of the European Recovery Program and by 1948 it depended on US material aid. [11] However, in 1947

the US government threatened to terminate this aid if there was a 'Communist victory' in 1948. [12] In

his Marshall Plan speech in June 1947, G. Marshall, declared that if "political parties… which…

perpetuate human misery" took power in recipient countries, ERP aid to those nations would be

terminated. [13] This economic coercion was articulated after the Truman administration declared that

$227 million was appropriated for interim aid, and would be sent to Italy to help redress its post-war

recession but only following a 'Communist' defeat in the election. [14] This put pressure on the FP,

leading to internal divisions, [15] and influenced the opinion of Italian voters, who realised that a left-

wing victory would be economically devastating. [16] Additionally, as the Soviets did not want parties

affiliated to them to receive Marshall aid, this exacerbated the splits within the FP. [17] Umberto

Terracini, co-leader of the PCI, argued that the ERP was fundamental for Italy's development.[18]

[11] Miller, *The United*, 213,

[12] James Clement Dunn to George C. Marshall, telegram, March 16, 1948, accessed March 14, 2017, https://history.state.gov/historicaldocuments/frus1948v03/d526

[13] George Catlett Marshall, "The Marshall Plan Speech," speech, June 1947, marshallfoundation.org, accessed February 21, 2017, http://marshallfoundation.org/marshall/the-marshall-plan/marshall-plan-speech/

[14] Stefano Luconi, "Anticommunism, Americanization, and Ethnic Identity: Italian Americans and the 1948 Parliamentary Elections in Italy," *The Historian* 62, no. 2 (2000): https://www.questiaschool.com/read/1G1-60578630/anticommunism-americanization-and-ethnic-identity

[15] Alessandro Brogi, *Confronting America: The Cold War between the United States and the Communists in France and Italy* (Chapel Hill, NC: University of North Carolina Press, 2011), 91, https://www.questiaschool.com/read/121593351/confronting-america-the-cold-war-between-the-united

[16] Ibid, 97

[17] Ibid, 91

[18] Ibid, 92

Indeed, the US government also supported the DC through covert CIA operations and other economic inducements. [19] Millions of dollars were channeled to the DC between 1947 and 1948; for instance, on 8th January 1947, the US government released $50 million to De Gasperi. [20] The US used its economic power to threaten supporters of the FP and to show that a left-wing victory would be economic suicide. The US also ensured that the DC had adequate resources to pursue a comprehensive propaganda campaign of its own. [21] Furthermore, the US government encouraged American Labor Unions, comprising of members of Italian descent, to send funds to anti-Communist parties in Italy. One influential union was the Ladies Garment Workers Union, which numbered 40,000 Italian members [22] and provided the Social Democratic Party, which split from its radical faction in 1947, with $200,000 for its election campaign. [23] These funds allowed Italian parties to make investments in anti-left propaganda, which was key to manipulating public opinion. The economic aid provided to Italy allowed the US to position itself as the only power that could lead the nation out of crisis [24] and this enabled it to manipulate voters' opinions. [25] The US government was open about its alignment with the DC and with De Gasperi. On 31st May 1947, after De Gasperi

---

[19] "Case Study: Italian Elections and CIA Founding," in *Understanding the hidden side of government*, ed. Loch K. Johnson, vol. 1, *Strategic Intelligence* (Praeger Security International, 2006), 37-38, accessed February 28, 2017, https://books.google.co.uk/books?id=cg39hcj6AxQC&pg=RA2-PA37&lpg=RA2-PA37&dq=cia+payments+to+italian+democratic+party+1948&source=bl&ots=QHIkmVNvo_&sig=0pnF54Brr6bAKdf6pgkNKJNxa18&hl=en&sa=X&ved=0ahUKEwifvZb8oLPSAhWqAMAKHVIVAE8Q6AEIODAF#v=onepage&q

[20] Miller, *The United*, 248

[21] "Case Study" 37-38

[22] Luconi, "Anticommunism, Americanization"

[23] Ibid

[24] Blum, *Killing Hope*, 30-31

[25] Miller, "Taking off the Gloves"

returned from a business trip to the US, he excluded left-wing parties from his coalition. [26] This was explained as a recommendation from the Truman administration which in return offered increased financial aid and cancelled the Italian debt to the US of $1 billion. [27]

Additionally, the US government was able to use the Roman Catholic Church as a tool of anti-left propaganda. [28] As Italy was predominantly Catholic, the Pope played a significant role in how political parties were portrayed. In January 1948, Pius XII asked the archbishop of New York for advice on how to approach the Italian political situation; the archbishop responded that the Pope should continue delivering anti-left speeches. [29] This was advice that Pius XII followed. [30] In one speech he made referencing the election the Pope declared "In this year of... threats... the time for Christian conscience has come". [31]

Furthermore, the US used the threat of military action to influence the outcome of the election. In February 1948, [32] the Truman administration laid contingency plans for military involvement in case of a left-wing victory. [33] This consisted of sending military aid to support underground operations in Italy to counter Communist forces. [34] Additionally, during the campaign, US warships were often

[26] Blum, *Killing Hope*, 29

[27] Miller, *The United*, 214

[28] Blum, *Killing Hope*, 30

[29] Brogi, *Confronting America*, 103
[30] Ibid

[31] Pius XII Pope, "Discorso Di Sua Santità Al Popolo Romano," speech, March 28, 1948, w2.vatican, accessed May 14, 2017, http://w2.vatican.va/content/pius-xii/it/speeches/1948/documents/hf_p-xii_spe_19480328_popolo-romano.html

[32] "Secret 1948 Role Disclosed by the U.S.," *The New York Times*, February 11, 1948, accessed May 14, 2017, https://www.cia.gov/library/readingroom/docs/CIA-RDP85B00236R000100150005-3.pdf

[33] Miller, "Taking off the Gloves"

[34] Noam Chomsky, "Restoring the Traditional Order," in *What Uncle Sam Really Wants* (n.p.: Odonian Press, 1992)

found anchored in Italian ports. [35] Indeed, military intimidations persuaded many Italians to vote for

the DC as there was no public appetite for another conflict that would throw Italy into crisis. [36]

However, it could be argued that US intervention in the Italian election did not determine its

outcome and that the key factor was the weakness of the FP. The exclusion of left-wing parties from

De Gasperi's cabinet [37] undermined their political credibility. Additionally, the FP failed to gain

assurance of economic support from the USSR that could counter US threats to remove aid. [38]

Indeed the FP's campaign also attacked the Marshall Plan and the Church, which proved deeply

unpopular, [39] as by 1948 most Italians were pro-American and pro-Roman Catholic. Pietro Secchia,

co-leader of the PCI, [40] stated that the US was the "organizer of sabotage and betrayal." [41] Historian

Alessandro Brogi argues that the FP's anti-Marshall campaign was disastrous as it threatened

"economic promise" and recovery. [42]

---

[35] Blum, *Killing Hope*, 31

[36] National Security Council, NSC 5/2, (Wash. 1948). Accessed May 14, 2017.
https://history.state.gov/historicaldocuments/frus1948v04/d28

[37] Blum, *Killing Hope*, 29

[38] Brogi, *Confronting America*, 92-97

[39] Miller, "Taking off the Gloves"

[40] Robert Ventresca, *From Fascism to Democracy: Culture and Politics in the Italian Election of 1948* (2004), 174,
accessed March 11, 2017,
https://books.google.co.uk/books?id=OKA6i7SenW0C&pg=PA168&lpg=PA168&dq=weaknesses+of+the+PCI+in+1948&s
ource=bl&ots=BNYTV0L9aa&sig=FHiuigJieiNTkT8wrellfuT9YZY&hl=it&sa=X&ved=0ahUKEwiD7uuI487SAhWIJ8AK
Hc1bBpYQ6AEIMDAC#v=onepage&q=
[41] Brogi, *Confronting America*, 104

[42] Ibid, 87

In addition, although divisions within the FP were exacerbated by US intervention, it was already deeply divided and its popularity was diminishing. When the coalition was established, a faction of the PSI split from the Socialist Party [43] and this undermined its stability. Historian James Miller argues that the FP was in a state of complete chaos by 1940. [44] The FP was unable to secure adequate funding to compete with the DC in terms of propaganda. Then, on March 20th 1948, after a declaration on the status of Trieste by Britain, France and the US, which called for the return of the area to Italian administration, Stalin opposed it and took Yugoslavia's side. [45] This was a death blow politically for the PCI as it became the party associated with a power that opposed historic Italian territorial interests. [46]

Finally, historian Robert Ventresca claims that the inherent strengths of the DC may have been the deciding factor in its victory. [47] The party invested effectively in its propaganda and relentlessly depicted the FP as 'godless'. [48] De Gasperi's ability as a leader was also exploited. Ventresca argues that De Gasperi was "indispensable to his... party" as he capably managed disparate groups within it. [49] In addition, it was De Gasperi who invited the Church's attacks on Communism and manipulated

---

[43] Miller, *The United,* 220

[44] Ibid

[45] Miller, "Taking off the Gloves"

[46] Ibid

[47] Robert Ventresca, *In God's Country: State, Society and Democracy in the Italian Election of 1948* (National Library of Canada, 2000), accessed March 14, 2017, http://www.collectionscanada.gc.ca/obj/s4/f2/dsk2/ftp03/NQ49908.pdf

[48] Ventresca, *From Fascism,* 200

[49] Ventresca, *In God's,* 70

the pulpit to depict the choice of April 1948 as one between 'Christianity and atheism'. [50] This led

voters to believe they needed to put their faith first at the ballot box. [51]

In conclusion, the weaknesses of the FP, De Gasperi's leadership and the support of the Catholic

Church for the DC were crucial factors in determining the outcome of the Italian general election of

1948. It is however reasonable to conclude that the extensive intervention of the US government,

through economic incentives and assistance, was a major factor in persuading Italians to vote for the

Christian Democrats. On 18th April 1948, Italians voted primarily to retain US economic support. The

threat of the cessation of ERP aid and of economic crisis, ultimately led to the FP's defeat.

Criteria C: Reflection

This investigation allowed me to better understand the methods used by historians.

I learned that there are obstacles when gathering a range of sources, and that accessing sensitive

primary material can be difficult. Although the Cold War has been written about extensively by

historians, the specific focus of my investigation was less well explored. As historians do, I had to

infer and cross reference material from experts, and CIA and military reports. It was also interesting

to see how historians reassess their perspectives when sources become available. Historian

Alessandro Brogi published his work in 2011 [52] and could access sources restricted up to the 1990s

which allowed him to write a more balanced account of events.

---

[50] Miller, *The United*, 248

[51] Ventresca, *In God's*, 3

[52] Blum, *Killing Hope*, 4

Selectivity is another challenge for historians and one I encountered in my investigation. As I developed my thematic arguments, I had to omit evidence such as details about exchanges of information between the US government and De Gasperi. I also had to be selective with secondary sources, and focused on the work of peer assessed, respected historians such as Noam Chomsky. Another obstacle highlighted to me was the potential cultural differences of historians themselves that needs to be appreciated. I worked with both English and Italian sources which revealed nuances in interpretations, particularly regarding religious-cultural factors. There are also challenges in the specialization of a historian; it was in fact difficult for me to interpret the economic data from the time as this is an area I do not study.

The need to evaluate sources was also highlighted to me as a key part of the historian's methodology, for example when using the CIA report titled 'Prospects for Communist Action in Italy'[53] as its content had to be assessed in line with the document's intent within the early Cold War context. Historian William Blum argues that US intervention led the DC to triumph,[54] while historian James Miller argues that the FP lost the election primarily due to its inherent weaknesses.[55] Both historians used similar evidence, but support different claims and this revealed how the use of reason and emotion is important in historians' methodology and how sources are interpreted; Historian Alessandro Brogi was born in Florence and was educated in Italy[56] and may have been influenced by national sentiments at the time when developing his account.

---

[53] Central Intelligence Agency, 54. *Weekly*

[54] Blum, *Killing Hope*, 27-34

[55] Miller, *The United*

[56] "Faculty Bio - Alessandro Brogi." uark.edu. Accessed March 9, 2017.
http://uark.edu/depts/histinfo/history/index.php/faculty_bio/2